The Complete Book on
HAND EVALUATION
In Contract Bridge

Mike Lawrence

Published by
Devyn Press, Inc.
Louisville, Kentucky

FIRST PRINTING   JUNE 1983
SECOND PRINTING   SEPTEMBER 1983
THIRD PRINTING   OCTOBER 1984
FOURTH PRINTING   JANUARY 1986
FIFTH PRINTING   MAY 1987
SIXTH PRINTING   MAY 1988
SEVENTH PRINTING   JULY 1989
EIGHTH PRINTING   JANUARY 1991
NINTH PRINTING   NOVEMBER 1993
TENTH PRINTING   SEPTEMBER 1996
ELEVENTH PRINTING   APRIL 2000

Printed in the United States of America.

Published by
Devyn Press
3600 Chamberlain Lane, Suite 230
Louisville, KY 40241
1-800-274-2221

Library of Congress No. 84-223827
ISBN 0-939460-27-0

Books by Mike Lawrence

HOW TO READ YOUR OPPONENTS' CARDS
Prentice Hall — 1973

WINNING BACKGAMMON
Pinnacle — 1975

JUDGMENT AT BRIDGE
Max Hardy — 1976

THE COMPLETE BOOK ON OVERCALLS IN CONTRACT BRIDGE
Max Hardy — 1980

TRUE BRIDGE HUMOR
Max Hardy — 1980

THE COMPLETE BOOK ON BALANCING IN CONTRACT BRIDGE
Max Hardy — 1981

PLAY A SWISS TEAM OF FOUR WITH MIKE LAWRENCE
Max Hardy — 1982

DYNAMIC DEFENSE
Devyn Press — 1982

MAJOR SUIT RAISES
Texas Bridge Supplies — 1982

THE COMPLETE BOOK ON HAND EVALUATION IN CONTRACT BRIDGE
Max Hardy — 1983

PLAY BRIDGE WITH MIKE LAWRENCE
Devyn Press — 1984

FALSE CARDS
Devyn Press — 1986

CARD COMBINATIONS
Devyn Press – 1986

SCRABBLE
Bantam Press — 1987

MIKE LAWRENCE'S WORKBOOK ON THE TWO OVER ONE SYSTEM
Max Hardy — 1987

PASSED HAND BIDDING
Lawrence & Leong – 1989

BIDDING QUIZZES, THE UNCONTESTED AUCTION
Lawrence & Leong — 1990

THE COMPLETE GUIDE TO CONTESTED AUCTIONS
Lawrence & Leong — 1992

TOPICS ON BRIDGE
Lawrence — 1990

MORE TOPICS ON BRIDGE
Lawrence — 1992

TABLE OF CONTENTS

INTRODUCTION

This is not the ordinary bridge book, nor is Mike Lawrence the ordinary bridge writer. It's a book for experienced bridge players, written by one of the best bridge minds of our generation.

That doesn't mean that you'll find it tough going. In fact, once you start to read the book, you'll have trouble putting it down. But that first perusal, enjoyable though it will be, is just the beginning. Give yourself a day or two to attend to a few chores, such as earning a living or paying some attention to your spouse, and then start to read it again.

After your second (or third) reading, you'll find that you know what Lawrence means and that you're ready to apply his teaching to your regular bridge game, whether that's rubber or tournament bridge. You don't have to make your partner read this book with you: it will improve your results quite apart from anything your various partners know about bidding. (And it's not a disadvantage at rubber bridge to raise the level of your own game while everybody else stands still.)

Instead of reading this book you might sit down and listen to Mike Lawrence talk for a few dozen hours. The subject doesn't matter, as long as he's talking about bridge. That will cost you a few thousand dollars, and you'll need a tape recorder to make sure you don't miss any of the golden words. A better way is to read one of his books. If you miss a few words you can glance back a few paragraphs or a few pages. And it will cost you only a few bucks.

Reading any Lawrence book is like listening to him talk. If you're any kind of decent bridge player, you're bound to profit by the experience. Reading this book is a special experience.

Evaluation, you'll find, is a very special subject. You can't become a really fine bidder unless you know what your hand is worth. On a high level, that means quite a bit more than counting your points. As you know, the truly great players don't rely solely on points to judge the value of a hand. They also think about *good* points and *bad* points, about the special value of aces, about the usefulness of tens and nines, about how their distribution affects their point count. When you've read this book you'll think the same way. You'll also think about *boxes* and *shell* points, two exotic additions to your bridge lingo.

To make a long story short, I envy you the pleasure of reading this book for the first time. But not very much, because I've already had the pleasure of reading it twice; and you may be quite sure that I'll go through it at least once more.

— ALFRED SHEINWOLD

FOREWORD

One of the most important things in any endeavor is the accumulation of experience and the ability to learn from it.

Most of the benefits of this experience can be described and put down in print so as to help others gain their experience. In fact, most areas of bridge have been covered in various volumes. There are very few questions one may have which have not somewhere been answered in print.

To my mind, any such question will be on bidding, and if it is a systemic question, some book out there has the answer.

The hard ones are questions of judgment where you have to decide whether or not to overcall or pass, to continue to game or sign off, to sit for the double, or to run. These are just a few of the typically hard decisions you must make.

There are some books which cover non-systemic areas of bidding. I even wrote a few of them. But there remains one underlying principle of bidding which is pertinent to all areas of bidding. It is the principle of evaluation which is the foundation for every close decision ever made at a bridge table.

Most players do not have much trouble with problems of evaluation when the auction goes, say,

1NT	Pass	2NT	Pass
?			

or perhaps

1♠	Pass	2♠	Pass
3♠	Pass	?	

These are auctions where the value of a given hand remains constant throughout the bidding. Compare them with these sequences.

1♣	Pass	1♠	Pass
2♠	Pass	3♦	Pass
?			

Responder has made a game try and opener must evaluate his hand in light of the three diamond bid.

1♣	Pass	1♠	Pass
2♠	Pass	3♥	Pass
?			

This time, opener has to evaluate his hand in light of a three heart bid. It is possible that on one of these sequences opener would jump to game, and would sign off with the other.

Try this. You have Q 7 2 of clubs. What is it worth?

If you are the opener, your Q 7 2 of clubs is an unknown value. You assign it two points in deference to its potential.

But what is it worth on any of the following sequences? Even when it isn't your bid, you should have some sense of value for your hand, or in this case, the Q 7 2 of clubs specifically.

LHO	Partner	RHO	You
1 ♠	1NT	Pass	?

LHO	Partner	RHO	You
1 ♣	Pass	2 ♣	?

LHO	Partner	RHO	You
Pass	1 ♣	Pass	?

LHO	Partner	RHO	You
Pass	1 ♣	Pass	1 ♡
Pass	2 ♣	Pass	?

LHO	Partner	RHO	You
Pass	1 ♣	Pass	1 ♡
Pass	3 ♣	Pass	?

LHO	Partner	RHO	You
Pass	1 ♠	Double	?

In each of these sequences, you should have experienced a sense of value of the Q 7 2 of clubs and it remains to be seen how far you should change your estimate as the auction changes.

In my opinion, the value of this Q 7 2 varies from as little as zero, or even minus, to as much as a healthy six or seven.

How come so much? Or so little? We'll see.

Chapter I

EVALUATING COMMON HOLDINGS

Before getting into specific hands, I want to take a look at a number of common holdings which are subject to problems of reevaluation. I will present a card combination followed by various auctions and will look to see how the value of that combination varies from sequence to sequence.

SINGLETON ACE

◊ A

You have the singleton ace of diamonds.

LHO opens *1 Diamond*. It is nice to have the diamond ace, and if we play in a suit, a stiff ace is a good holding. But as aces go, I would prefer to have a different ace. If we defend, the diamond ace is a sure trick and its being singleton suggests the suit will divide poorly for declarer. If we play the hand, it will be useful, whether we play at notrump or at a suit. However, since LHO opened 1 ◊, there is not much chance that the ace of diamonds will help to establish *additional* tricks.

Most players realize that kings, queens, jacks, and even tens fare much better when they are accompanied by other honors. A king with no accompanying honors may take a trick. Likewise a queen. But look what happens when you start combining honors rather than leaving them stranded.

K x x x opposite x x = ½ trick
Q x x x opposite x x = ¼ trick
J x x x opposite x x is almost worthless
10 x x x opposite x x is worthless

These combinations in total are worth less than one trick.

But start combining these honors in various combinations and we have these approximations.

Q J x x opposite x x = ¾ trick
K J x x opposite x x = ¾ trick
K Q x x opposite x x = 1½ tricks
Q J 10 x opposite x x = at least 1 trick
K J 10 x opposite x x = at least 1½ tricks

all the way up to

K Q J 10 opposite x x = 3 tricks

1

This principle can be extended to include aces as well. This fact is not as well appreciated as it should be though, perhaps because the ace itself always wins a trick.

Here are some typical situations.

♠ x x x	Let's assume spades are divided 3-2. Your normal
♡ A x x	play is to lead to the king of spades. If the ace is on-
□	side, you get three spade tricks and a heart. Four
♠ K x x x x	tricks. If the spade is offside, you get two spades
♡ x	and a heart. Three tricks.

Now change the situation a little.

♠ A x x	If spades are still 3-2, you have four sure tricks. If
♡ x x x	spades are 4-1 or 5-0, the net effect will still be that
□	the ace of spades is worth one half trick more than
♠ K x x x x	the ace of hearts, thus demonstrating that even aces
♡ x	can vary in value. If an isolated ace is worth four

points, then one which adds ½ trick to the hand should be worth six.

And it could be even worse. Change the situation one more time to this.

♠ x x	Now, the ace of hearts is not even worth one trick.
♡ A x x x x	You can take a trick with it, but you will still have
□	to lose some number of spades. Effectively, if you
♠ K x x x x x	take the ace of hearts, you will have to throw a
♡ —	spade on it, and that spade is ultimately going to be

a winner in its own right. In the above setup, if spades are 3-2, you will win three or four tricks. If the heart ace were the spade ace, you would win five — an enormous difference. Using the point count evaluation, the ace of hearts would be worth zero and the ace of spades from eight to twelve.

Compare these two similar hands:

Combination #1	*Combination #2*
♠ 4 2	♠ A 2
♡ K 8 7 6 5	♡ K 8 7 6 5
◇ A Q J 4	◇ A Q J 4
♣ A 3	♣ 4 3
□	□
♠ K 7 5	♠ K 7 5
♡ A Q 9 4 2	♡ A Q 9 4 2
◇ K 10 5 2	◇ K 10 5 2
♣ 5	♣ 5

The first pair of hands makes six hearts if the spade finesse wins. An even chance. But the second hand with the same apparent values is cold for six hearts. Quite a difference.

Continuing with the singleton ace of diamonds, there are additional minus factors to consider.

It is inflexible. If you play the hand and they lead this suit, you will not be able to exercise any judgment as to when or where to win the trick.

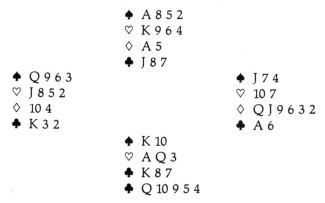

```
                    ♠ A 8 5 2
                    ♡ K 9 6 4
                    ◊ A
                    ♣ J 8 7 5
    ♠ Q 9 6 3                      ♠ J 7 4
    ♡ J 8 5 2                      ♡ 10 7
    ◊ 10 4                         ◊ Q J 9 6 3 2
    ♣ K 3 2                        ♣ A 6
                    ♠ K 10
                    ♡ A Q 3
                    ◊ K 8 7 5
                    ♣ Q 10 9 4
```

West leads the diamond ten against three notrump. When West gets in with the king of clubs, he will lead his second diamond. East's diamonds will be set up too soon for declarer to establish his clubs.

Compare the last hand with the following hand.

```
                    ♠ A 8 5 2
                    ♡ K 9 6 4
                    ◊ A 5
                    ♣ J 8 7
    ♠ Q 9 6 3                      ♠ J 7 4
    ♡ J 8 5 2                      ♡ 10 7
    ◊ 10 4                         ◊ Q J 9 6 3 2
    ♣ K 3 2                        ♣ A 6
                    ♠ K 10
                    ♡ A Q 3
                    ♠ K 8 7
                    ♣ Q 10 9 5 4
```

In this setup, West again leads the ten of diamonds against three notrump. But this time, declarer is able to effect a holdup. By ducking the first trick, and winning the second, declarer is able to keep the defense from establishing the diamonds in time.

◊ A

LHO	Partner	RHO	You
1◊	1♠	Pass	?

As noted before, it is nice to have the ace of diamonds, but it is not necessarily a wonderful thing. If you play the hand, and get a diamond lead, you will win the first trick, but if partner wants to ruff diamonds in your hand, he won't be able to do it immediately.

For instance.

♠ K 8 7
♡ 8 6 5 4 2
♢ A
♣ 10 7 6 4
□
♠ Q J 10 6 4 2
♡ A 10
♢ 9 6 3
♣ K Q

Playing in four spades, you get a diamond lead. If you could ruff two diamonds in dummy, four spades would be easy. In this hand however, you may not be able to follow this line because the defense can play two rounds of spades.

Exchange the ace and three of diamonds, and it will be easy. Diamond ace, diamond ruff, heart ace, diamond ruff, concede a trump, etc. Ten easy tricks.

♢ A

LHO	Partner	RHO	You
1♢	1NT	Pass	?

Whatever else you may have to think about, you don't have to worry about diamond stoppers for notrump. However, you should still feel that a stiff ace is a flaw. Its lack of flexibility can hurt you in a number of ways. First, you won't have the option of holding up (see previous hands). And secondly, you may not be able to develop additional tricks in the suit.

A   A   A
□   □   □
K J 9 7   Q 10 6 4   J 10 7 3

In all of these cases, LHO leads a small card losing to the ace. Now, if the defense is so inclined, they may refrain from leading this suit again. Consequently, you may end up with only two tricks in the first case, and one trick in the remaining cases.

Now look what happens when you add a small card to the ace.

A 2	A 2	A 2
□	□	□
K J 9 7	Q 10 6 4	J 10 7 3

When LHO leads the suit, you are assured of three tricks in the first case and two tricks in each of the others. And if you go one step further and give dummy a third card, then you have the potential to win four tricks in case one and three in case two.

A curious point here. Say you have one of these combinations.

$$♡ \quad Q\ 10\ 8\ 2$$
$$♡ \quad K\ J\ 7$$
$$♡ \quad K\ 9\ 2$$

Whatever you decide they are worth, you will agree that if RHO opens the bidding with 1♡, the value of these combinations goes up. You would tend to rate them thusly.

♡ Q 10 8 2   worth two tricks for notrump.

♡ K J 7   also two tricks.

♡ K 9 2   one trick.

It is true that these estimates may fail, but they are reasonable. Now assume that you buy the contract in some number of notrump and your dummy provides the ace of this suit. Let's be generous and provide A x x.

A 4 3	A 4 3	A 4 3
□	□	□
Q 10 8 2	K J 7	K 9 2

In all of these cases, the presence of the ace added one trick to your expectations. This is not the usual increase in value when you add an ace into a suit combination.

Remember, if you have K 9 2 of a suit, you think of it as half a trick. If partner has the ace, you now have two tricks, an increase of one and a half tricks. But when RHO opens the bidding, you think of your K 9 2 as a full trick, so when partner produces the ace, the increase in your expectations is one trick rather than one and a half. Similarly, when you have K J 7 and no information, you think of it as ¾ of a trick. If partner has the ace, the combination will be worth 2½ tricks, an increase of 1¾ tricks. But if RHO opens the bidding in this suit, you hope your K J 7 to be two tricks, so the presence of the ace in dummy adds only one trick to your evaluation.

ACE DOUBLETON AND ACE THIRD

When you start adding small cards so that you have A x or A x x, things start to change, sometimes significantly. At notrump contracts, you will always find those little cards are a distinct blessing. If the opponents are attempting to set up the suit, you will be able to control the tempo. And if you are trying to set up the suit, those small cards will make an easy task out of an impossible one.

A	A 2	A 3 2
□	□	□
K J 7 6 5	K J 7 6 5	K J 7 6 5

With the first holding, you will have to have both entries and luck to come to four tricks. Three tricks is your likely result and that will require South to have three side entries. The second setup provides a slight chance of five tricks and four will not require enormous good fortune. And should you have a third card in dummy, you will score five tricks fairly frequently, and four will be the rule rather than the exception.

This implies that when you are evaluating your hand, it is not sufficient that you pay attention only to your high cards. It is certainly true that high cards can fluctuate in value, but a large part of their value will be a result of the small cards.

When the opponents have bid a suit and you are contemplating playing in a suit contract, A x or A x x of the opponent's suit offer different considerations.

◊ A x

LHO	Partner	RHO	You
1◊	1♠	Pass	?

Compared to other holdings you might have, A x is quite good. You have sure control of the suit and are not in danger of two fast losers. Any other holding not headed by the ace is subject to either being led through or being ruffed off. For instance

◊ K x x   They may be able to grab three fast tricks.

◊ K J x   They may be able again to take three tricks. Perhaps one or more of them will be ruffing.

◊ K Q J 9   It is possible to lose as many as four diamond tricks if RHO has a stiff.

6

◇ A x

LHO	Partner	RHO	You
1◇	1♠	2◇	?

On sequences where an opponent has raised, the worst length you can have in their suit is two and even though you have the ace, it is not that useful a holding. For one thing, the ace is almost certainly the "wrong" ace. You would far rather have that ace elsewhere.

LENGTH IN THE OPPONENT'S SUIT

Throughout these discussions, I will be making references to certain suit length concepts. This is one of them.

Rule. When an opponent opens with a one bid, the worst length you can have in his suit is three. This is because three cards is the length most likely to maximize the number of losers you have in their suit. If you have one or two cards in their suit, you cannot lose more than one or two tricks. If you have four or more, your partner may have a doubleton, again holding your losers to two. But if you have three, there is no particular reason to expect partner to have two or less, thus opening the possibility of having three losers.

Rule. When an opponent opens with a one bid and is raised, the worst number of cards you can have in their suit is two. As in the previous discussion, the reason this length is bad is that it maximizes the number of losers you may have in the suit. If you had a singleton, you would expect to have one loser. But if you had three or more, you could hope partner had only one. Even if partner did not have a singleton, but produced a doubleton, you could count on ruffing your third card in partner's hand.

The worst of all cases is when you and your partner have perfectly matching distributions. If you each have, say 5-3-2-3 distributions in exactly that order, then there is no ruffing trick available to your side. This is an additional reason to fear three cards in their suit when it hasn't been raised, or a doubleton when it has been raised. Sometimes in fact, there will be a highly competitive auction where you have a singleton in their suit and you can judge that partner also has one. This is a rare situation, but if it occurs, you should be aware that this matching distribution will not be to your benefit.

◇ A x x

LHO	Partner	RHO	You
1◇	1♠	Pass	?

You start with the worst length possible. The opening lead can easily

7

establish two tricks for the defense. There is the likelihood that partner has no values in diamonds in which case there is no additional combinative value. Even if partner does have a diamond card which combines with the ace, there is little chance of developing a long trick.

◇ A x x

LHO	Partner	RHO	You
1 ◇	1 ♠	2 ◇	?

With the opponents bidding and raising diamonds, this holding becomes rather useful. It would not be surprising to find partner with one or two small diamonds. It's true that there will be no additive value to the ace, but against that, you will have one or no losers in the suit.

◇ A
◇ A x
◇ A x x

LHO	Partner	RHO	You
1 ♡	1 ♠	2 ♡	?

These three combinations are in a suit as yet unbid by either side. You should tend to look fondly on these holdings. There is no guarantee, but perhaps partner has some side values or even a second suit of the sort which will combine with your respective holding. This is a potential thing only; but it implies that these holdings are better than if they were in the suit bid by the opponents, *i.e.*, hearts.

♡ A
♡ A x
♡ A x x

LHO	Partner	RHO	You
1 ◇	1 ♡	2 ◇	?

With partner bidding hearts, your heart ace significantly increases in value. The stiff ace of hearts has limited value because it has no additional length but it will combine to help establish partner's suit. Certainly, you would prefer to have A x x.

Other ace high combinations are worth considering — A J x, A Q x, A Q, A K, A K x, etc.

◇ A K x

LHO	Partner	RHO	You
1 ◇	1 ♠	Pass	?

As usual, values in the opponent's suit have as little value as possible relative to what they would be worth if they were in an unbid suit or in partner's suit. Remember, values in the opponent's suit are not likely to find high cards in partner's hand to combine with and there is not much chance of developing little cards in the suit. Values in unbid suits *may* be opposite some length and strength in partner's hand, so can have added value. And values in partner's suit are guaranteed on all counts.

◇ A Q x

LHO	Partner	RHO	You
1◇	1♠	Pass	?

When it looks like the lead is going to come through your A Q of diamonds, you should feel that the queen is of no value. Far better to have the lead coming to your hand. Suit combinations headed by the ace have a quality unlike any other combinations in that you can get a trick any time you want. You are not subject to defensive maneuvers such as the holdup. Your ace, if you play the hand from your side, offers you two tempos. One, LHO can't attack immediately, and two, if RHO gets in to lead the suit, you can win immediately. Hopefully, you will have had time to set up discards.

In any case, you would generally prefer your A Q x to be elsewhere.

THE DIFFERENCE BETWEEN ACE HIGH AND OTHER COMBINATIONS.

So far, this discussion has been limited to ace high combinations and what makes them good or bad. This is because they are so different from all other combinations that they must be considered as separate cases.

Before getting into other combinations, I want to take a look at some of the differences.

1. An ace is a trick, regardless of the bidding.

A x x   K J x
□   □
x x x   x x x

Whatever else happens, the first combination is a trick. The second combination may actually be worth two tricks, but it may be worth none.

2. An ace is timing.

A x x   K Q x
□   □
x x x   x x x

In the first case, you can win the ace at your convenience. In the second case, you are subject to the whims of the opponents.

3. An ace is less subject to being ruffed off.

A J x x	K J x x
□	□
Q 10 x x	Q 10 x x

In the first case, you can win the ace, draw trumps, and later concede a loser in this suit. In the second case, the defense may be able to get the ace plus three ruffs.

4. An ace is control.

A x x	K Q J
□	□
x x x x	x x x x

Perhaps you have sufficient tricks that you can win the ace in case one and take later discards. In case two, you have a fast loser plus possible ruffs.

It is clear that ace high combinations can have some flaws, but they are minor compared to the disasters that can befall other combinations.

The reason other combinations have such a wide range of values is that they are subject to such factors as location, *i.e.* over or under the bidder, and being ruffed off.

Chapter II

COMMON EVALUATION SITUATIONS

Here is a list of common circumstances which offer different problems of evaluation.

1. You are the dealer.
2. LHO opens the bidding with one of a suit.
3. LHO opens and RHO raises.
4. LHO opens one notrump.
5. Partner opens one notrump.
6. LHO opens with one of a suit and partner overcalls one notrump.
7. LHO opens with a suit bid and partner doubles.
8. Partner opens one of a suit.
9. Partner opens and rebids his suit.
10. RHO opens with one of a suit.
11. RHO opens and LHO raises.
12. RHO opens one notrump.
13. Partner overcalls

1. *You are the dealer.*

This is what you might term the neutral position. At this stage, you have no real indication of what your hand is worth and for want of anything better, you assign some amount of value to each of your high cards. A king is worth three, a queen two, etc. Of note is that you should already be doing some reevaluating to recognize such factors as whether your honors are in your long or short suits. Are they reinforcing each other? Do you have spots or do you have deuces and treys? For example

♠ A 7		♠ 10 3
♡ K 6 4		♡ 10 8 5
◇ Q J 3 2	vs.	◇ A K Q 10
♣ Q 7 6 3		♣ Q J 9 5

You should feel that the second twelve-point hand is worth two or three points more than the first.

2. *LHO opens the bidding with one of a suit.*
   There are two sub cases here.

   First, you can have honors in the suit bid by opener.
   Second, you can have honors in the unbid suits.

As far as honors in the unbid suits go, you should not feel that they are bad. It is true that LHO is likely to have high cards over your high cards, but unless opener later shows extra strength, you should not worry.

But if you are looking at honors in opener's suit, you should feel some concern. One thing you should not do, however, is to completely discount them. This would be excessive. If you have one of the following holdings

K J x x
K x x
Q x x
Q J x
etc.

you are entitled to downgrade the value of these holdings. But consider this. We have all opened 1 ♣ on x x x a few times in our lives and we have all opened 1 ♡ or 1 ♠ on 10 x x x x on occasion. Opener won't always have the missing high cards.

Rule. Until partner shows shortness in the opponent's suit, or until the opponents' bidding tells you partner is short, you should only partially devaluate these holdings. What you have lost is twofold, but neither is totally fatal . . . yet.

   a. LHO's bid suggests he has high cards over you.
   b. LHO's bid suggests that neither you nor partner will have useful
      small cards in that suit.

Here's an example:

K 10 7
□
Q 6 5 4 2

You know you can establish one trick via force, and you hope to establish as many as three additional tricks with the little cards.

But if RHO had opened the bidding in this suit, your chances of establishing the little cards will be slight. If RHO has a four-bagger, you can set up one length trick, but if he has all five, you will get one trick only, assuming no endplay or misdefense.

It is important to appreciate the value of these length tricks that are no longer available to your side. When you start life with Q 8 7 of a suit, it is awarded two points in recognition of its potential. By itself, a queen is hardly worth two points.

x x

□

Q x x

Unless partner comes up with something, it will be nearly worthless. Partner can have all manner of holdings.

	He can have
Q 8 7	K J 3
	K J 4 2
	K J 9 6 4 2
	J 10 3
	J 10 6 4
	A K 6 3
	A K J 4 3 2
	9 2

Sometimes that queen is worth one trick, sometimes no tricks, sometimes two or more. Sometimes it helps to set up some high-card tricks as when it is opposite K J 3. Sometimes it helps to set up long-suit tricks, as when opposite J 10 6 4. It is the total of all these situations which serve to give the queen an original value of two points. If you suddenly take away from its potential the ability to set up long-suit tricks, it is just as much a decrease in the value of the queen as if you lessened the chance of setting up high-card tricks.

3. *LHO opens and RHO raises.*

When this happens, you should take as gloomy a view as possible toward honors in their suits. There are three separate situations to consider:

    a. You can have a stiff in their suit.
    b. You can have a doubleton in their suit.
    c. You can have three or more in their suit.

When you have a stiff king or queen, you should treat it as a singleton only in value and should be intensely disapppointed that it was the king or queen.

Rule. Any wasted high cards you may have are not only worthless, but they are a minus as well.

When they bid 1 ♠ -Pass-2 ♠, they will have usually a minimum of seventeen or eighteen high-card points. If they don't have them in

13

spades then they have them somewhere else. This means that for now, the maximum high cards available to your side will be twenty-two or twenty-three. If some of them are wasted, then your net will be as few as eighteen or nineteen.

Note that when a suit has been raised, your side's chances of setting up small cards is zero. First, you aren't likely to have any length in their suit, and even if so, you won't be able to set them up. When they raise, it is 100% that you won't be setting up long tricks, so that amount of potential is not available to any honors you have in their suit. And since there was a raise, that increases the chance that partner won't have an honor to combine with your honors. And even if he does, it won't be good for your side.

Say you have:

♠ Q 7 6 2
♡ K
♢ 8 6 5 4
♣ Q 8 6 3

It goes

LHO	Partner	RHO	You
1♡	1♠	2♡	2♠
Pass	Pass	Pass	

They lead a heart and surprise, the king wins. A good card? Should you be higher? Unlikely. Here is partner's hand.

♠ Q 7 6 2
♡ K
♢ 8 6 5 4
♣ Q 8 6 3
□
♠ A J 9 5 3
♡ A J 2
♢ K 9 3
♣ 9 2

With reasonable luck, you will make two, even three spades. But, one might be the limit.

Now let's change the heart king to the club king. We now have:

♠ Q 7 6 2
♡ 3
♢ 8 6 5 4
♣ K Q 6 3

Now with reasonable luck, you will make three or four spades. Your

14

heart king was a winner, but not a useful one. Both of declarer's hearts could be ruffed so that winning the heart king was of little consequence. Come to think of it, it is now possible to make five spades.

Now let's change the heart jack to the club jack. We have:

♠ Q 7 6 2
♡ 3
♢ 8 6 5 4
♣ K Q 6 3
□
♠ A J 9 5 3
♡ A 8 2
♢ K 9 3
♣ J 2

Now, while three could be the maximum, it would not be surprising to see four or even five spades coming home.

And finally, change the ace of hearts to the ace of diamonds, leaving this:

♠ Q 7 6 2
♡ 3
♢ 8 6 5 4
♣ K Q 6 3
□
♠ A J 9 5 3
♡ 10 8 2
♢ A K 3
♣ J 2

Now four spades is cold without a diamond lead, but is the favorite even so. I would expect par to be eleven tricks.

What has happened of course is that the sterile heart honors were transferred elsewhere where they could recognize their potential.

When RHO raises, and you have a doubleton in the opponents' suit, you start with the worst possible number of cards in that suit. When you throw in the king, queen, or jack, or various combinations of these cards, you create a genuine monster.

Say you have K x. With the opponents bidding and raising, the chances of partner having a helping card are minimized.

Say you have Q x. This is absolutely hopeless. If partner has nothing, you have two losers, and if partner has the ace or king, (unlikely), the queen will have no value anyway.

x x
□
K x x

If RHO has opened this suit, you will lose to the ace, cash your king, and can ruff your small card in dummy.

Q x
□
K x x

When you throw in the queen, it adds nothing or little to the combination. Only if LHO has the ace will you be happy you have the queen.

Here is another set of hands to show how wasted values in their suit are, even though they are winners.

LHO	Partner	RHO	You
1♡	Double	2♡	2♠
Pass	Pass	Pass	

These are your combined hands:

♠ A 10 7 3
♡ K 7 5
◇ Q 8 2
♣ A 10 5
□
♠ K 9 6 2
♡ Q J
◇ K 9 3 2
♣ J 9 3

These hands will likely make two spades, but down one is possible and making three is possible.

Changing things a little we get

♠ A 10 7 3
♡ K 7 5
◇ Q J 2
♣ A 10 5
□
♠ K 9 6 2
♡ Q 3
◇ K 9 3 2
♣ J 9 3

Now three is the favorite. The worthless jack of hearts has become a valuable jack of diamonds.

More changes, this time the heart queen to the spade queen.

♠ A Q 7 3
♡ K 7 5
◇ Q J 2
♣ A 10 5
□
♠ K 9 6 2
♡ 8 3
◇ K 9 3 2
♣ J 9 3

Four spades is now possible. But it could go down. Note that the king of hearts has some value here in that it will keep the heart losers to one. Even so, if the heart king were changed to the club king, it would be an improvement.

♠ A Q 7 3
♡ 9 7 5
◇ Q J 2
♣ A 10 5
□
♠ K 9 6 2
♡ 8 3
◇ K 9 3 2
♣ K J 9

Now you have two heart losers, but four spades will still make if diamonds are 3-3, the ten doubleton or if you can find the club queen. Of course, if spades divide 4-1, you are in trouble, but that's another problem.

You should especially note the original heart combination of K x x opposite Q J. It is typical of wasted cards. True, you got two tricks from the combination, but they were at the expense of three honor cards. They did combine with each other to produce two winners, but there was no promotion of small cards. I could have made it even worse. Say K x opposite Q J. Now you would have one trick.

So far, I feel that these comparisons have been rather mild. For instance, I have not given any five or six card suits which might have benefited from an additional card or two. I will correct this oversight shortly.

In this sequence, partner overcalls and then makes a game try by bidding three diamonds.

LHO	Partner	RHO	You
1♡	1♠	2♡	2♠
Pass	3◊	Pass	?

You hold:

♠ K 7 5
♡ K Q 8 7
◊ 5 4 2
♣ J 4 2

My impression of this hand is that it is worth three spades only and that this contract will be in jeopardy. No number of notrump would even come to mind. However, that is not the point of this discussion. The point is that your heart honors are nearly worthless.

♠ K 7 5
♡ K Q 8 7
◊ 5 4 2
♣ J 4 2

□

♠ Q J 10 8 3
♡ J
◊ A J 8 6 3
♣ A 5

It seems to me that partner has done well to stop in three spades. A good decision, which probably required some effort. Against good defense, he will probably go one down. A poor reward for his discipline. Perhaps you say he ought not to have made a game try? Opposite:

♠ K x x x
♡ x x x x
◊ K x
♣ x x x

four spades would be near laydown. No, I don't think the game try was out of order. If anything, the flaw in the auction was the raise to two spades. With K 7 5 of trumps the bid was certainly reasonable, and it would be made by everyone, but nonetheless, it was the bid that led to the problem.

Rather than go through a card by card change as I did in the previous two examples, I'll just make two minor changes.

♠ K 7 5 2
♡ 8 6 4
◇ Q 10 5
♣ 6 4 2

□

♠ Q J 10 8 3
♡ 2
◇ A J 8 6 3
♣ A 5

No king, queen, or jack of hearts. No jack of clubs. It is now possible that three spades is the limit, even down one on a diamond ruff, but against that, four or even five spades is possible if the defense fails to get after clubs in time. Quite a difference.

This hand very clearly shows the difference between wasted cards and pure working cards. The result of this hand would be the same even if those wasted cards were retrieved to produce this dummy:

♠ K 7 5 2
♡ K Q J
◇ Q 10 5
♣ J 4 2

Whatever the result of this hand, the heart and club honors in dummy will play no part.

Let me assure you of one thing. I have not gone to any lengths creating hands to make a point. The hands shown here were typical. It was no trouble at all to find them. They happen all the time.

Here is one last example, concocted I admit, to show the effect of consolidated honors in a short suit.

♠ K J 7 2
♡ A K Q
◇ A 4 2
♣ K 4 2

♠ A 6 5 4
♡ 8 6 5
◇ Q 8 6
♣ Q 8 5

Here you have the A K Q of hearts racing three small. Three sure winners. You also have three suits each with potential losers. If you were playing this hand in spades, you could end up losing tricks thusly.

Spades. You have half a loser if spades divide 3-2 and will have an additional loser if they are 4-1.

Hearts. No losers.

Diamonds. You have one and a half losers.

Clubs. You have two losers.

On a bad day if spades break poorly and you lose every finesse in sight, you could end up losing six tricks.

Now rearrange the high cards so that you have no holes in spades, diamonds, or clubs, and instead have three heart losers. This is what you get.

> ♠ K J 7 2
> ♡ 10 9 7
> ◇ A 4 2
> ♣ K 4 2
>
> □
>
> ♠ A Q 5 4
> ♡ 8 6 5
> ◇ K Q 6
> ♣ A Q 5

Three heart losers and that's it. Quite an improvement. Furthermore, adding the spade queen means you don't have to worry about 4-1 spades.

4. *LHO opens one notrump.*

When LHO opens one notrump, you will tend to take a dim view of any questionable holdings since there is slight chance that partner will have high cards to fit with yours. It is true that your holdings such as K J x or Q 10 5 can blossom when partner provides Q 10 8 x x or K J 9 x x x but the chances of this happening are far less than before the opening bid.

This doesn't mean that when LHO opens one notrump, you should always be discouraged. If partner can act, you will have a chance to reevaluate and may find that your dull hand becomes quite worthwhile. For example

LHO	Partner	RHO	You
1NT	2♣*	Pass	?

(*showing hearts and spades)

You hold

> ♠ K J 3
> ♡ K 4
> ◇ J 7 6 5
> ♣ 9 6 4 2

You would be quite justified in jumping to four spades on the basis of your major suit kings.

This is a better hand, high card wise, but two spades is enough.

$$♠ \ 8 \ 7 \ 5$$
$$♡ \ 7 \ 2$$
$$◇ \ K \ Q \ J \ 5$$
$$♣ \ K \ J \ 7 \ 4$$

Much more on this later.

5. *Partner opens one notrump.*

For the time being, you should feel that every honor in your hand is carrying its weight. If you have J 8 6, a holding not usually too well thought of, you should not discount it too readily. True, it might be worthless, but if partner comes up with Q 10 7 2, he will be quite pleased with your J 8 6. In this setting, your jack will be invaluable, working to set up a high card trick as well as a potential long trick. It is combinations like this one which justify counting the jack as one point.

| Q 10 7 2 | opposite | J 8 6 | Perhaps two tricks. |
| Q 10 7 2 | opposite | 8 6 3 | Who knows? You may get |

something out of this, but you will need entries to lead up to the Q 10 7 2. If you have no entries, you will have to lead away from the queen and will have to depend on a 3-3 break.

As good as that J 8 6 might turn out to be, if you have good spots or perhaps combined honors, they will be even more valuable. How often have you had a doggy six count like this one:

$$♠ \ Q \ J \ 8$$
$$♡ \ 9 \ 7$$
$$◇ \ Q \ J \ 8 \ 7 \ 5$$
$$♣ \ 10 \ 7 \ 5$$

Partner opened one notrump, you passed correctly, and watched as he took in ten fairly easy tricks. Turned out, it was cold and partner had only an average sixteen.

$$♠ \ A \ K \ 6 \ 2$$
$$♡ \ K \ 10 \ 3$$
$$◇ \ A \ 10 \ 4$$
$$♣ \ Q \ 8 \ 3$$

Not that three notrump was a good contract. It just happened to make.

When RHO overcalls partner's one notrump, things change. That J 8 6, which you were envisioning as a useful filler which might even help produce length tricks, changes dramatically in stature. After 1NT-2♣-? your spade J 8 6 immediately loses all of its length potential and it loses some of its honor value as well. It does retain value though in the sense that if partner has an honor in spades, your side will have a sure stopper. Note that if you had J 8 only, you might not be guaranteed that stopper as partner could hold K x or Q x.

6. *LHO opens with a suit bid and partner overcalls one notrump.*

When partner overcalls one notrump as opposed to opening one notrump, your evaluation of honors will run along similar lines as to when partner opens one notrump.

You will, however, take a slightly different view of honors in opener's suit.

Since LHO has bid the suit, you should discount these honors somewhat, even though they will contribute.

Firstly, there is diminished chance that they will contribute to length tricks. Of note here is that if the opening bid was one club or one diamond, then your partner may have length. Opener could have a three-card suit. But it is not guaranteed. If the opening bid was one heart or one spade, then partner is less likely to have length since opener tends to have five. This means that when the opening bid was a major suit, and partner bids one notrump, honors in that major will be worth less than if the opening bid was a minor and you had honors there instead.

Secondly, there are quite a few combinations where your honor card contributes nothing to the hand.

Here are a number of such situations viewed from the other side of the table. RHO in all cases has opened one spade and you have overcalled one notrump.

5 2
□
Q J 6 4

This looks like two stoppers with the suit having been bid on your right. It may or may not produce two tricks.

K 2
□
Q J 6 4

Adding the king to responder's hand guarantees you can take two tricks, but it does not increase the number of stoppers. If South had the eight, nine, or ten of spades, then the combination would be worth another stopper and perhaps a trick. Note that a trick and a stopper are not the same thing.

satisfaction. For the first time in this discussion, we have an auction where partner has promised, or at least implied, length and strength in all suits. Regardless of what honors you have,

J x
Q x x
K x x x

there is an excellent chance you will find partner with fitting high cards and potentially promotable small cards.

Compare this with when partner opened or overcalled 1NT. When this happened, you were able to count on your honors fitting with something in partner's hand, but you could only hope to find useful length as well. If you held Q 10 x of clubs and heard partner bid one notrump, you would like your club holding, but you would not know how much. Does partner have K x or A J 5 3? The length potential was unknown.

But when partner doubles 1 ♥ and you have Q 10 x of clubs, there is every reason to expect that you will be facing better than K x. True, partner may have an awkward hand and may have doubled with K x of clubs, but that would be rare. After the example sequence, 1 ♥ - double-pass-? I would rate this hand thusly.

♠ Q 10 8 2
♥ K J 5 3
◊ Q 3
♣ 10 4 2

This hand works out to about nine points, but that total is arrived at in this fashion.

♠ Q 10 8 2

I expect this to be worth around four points. Both the queen and ten, even perhaps the eight, are all working, and I have a fourth card in the suit partner is most looking for.

♥ K J 5 3

These are not going to be worth much, but if partner has the queen or even the ten, we may come to a couple of tricks. This is a far better holding than K J x. In an offhand sort of way, I consider the fourth card to be a winner in that I can anticipate ruffing it in dummy. I would rate this holding at a couple of points but only because of the fourth card.

◊ Q 3

Another greatly appreciated card. Partner claims to have something in diamonds, so the diamond queen will be useful. Note that when partner doubles, he tends to have four spades, although possibly three. Five spades would be exceptional because with most five-card spade suits, he would overcall instead. Minor suits are another story. Partner's double of one heart shows an interest in diamonds, but his holding can vary far more than his spade holding.

For example, these would all be doubles of 1♡.

♠ K J 4 2	♠ Q 10 4	♠ K J 7	♠ Q J 4
♡ 8 7	♡ 8 3	♡ 8 3	♡ 8 2
◊ 10 6 5	◊ K 8 6 4	◊ A K J 8 4	◊ Q J 8 6 5
♣ A K J 5	♣ A K J 5	♣ Q 10 3	♣ A K 5

By comparison, if the last two hands were changed to

♠ A K J 8 4	♠ Q J 8 6 5
♡ 8 3	♡ 8 2
◊ K J 7	◊ Q J 4
♣ Q 10 3	♣ A K 5

it would be better to overcall rather than double.

This suggests the diamond queen can range from worthless, opposite 10 6 5, to quite exceptional, opposite A K J 8 4. My opinion of the Q 3 of diamonds is still high, and I rate it on a par with the spade queen. The difference is that the spade queen is a proven value. Since the diamond queen will realize some of its potential, I feel it is worth about three points.

♣ 10 4 2

Three small is not a good holding but this one has the redeeming feature of the club ten. Partner has something in clubs so the ten can easily be worth something.

K J 7 3
□
10 4 2

You would rather the club ten were in the dummy with the K J, but it can still have an effect on the play in this suit.

Q 9 8 7
□
10 4 2

The ten doubles the number of tricks you can take in this suit. With it, you get two tricks if LHO has the jack.

Even if your holding were 4 3 2, it might not be so bad. Some of the time, three small can be the worst imaginable holding, but not always. It can also be a neutral holding and once in a while, an excellent holding. I will spend a lot of time on it in a separate section.

In the immediate case, you can treat x x x as neutral. Partner will have some club cards and with luck they will be working. LHO has strength so he may have the missing club cards. This is only a marginal assumption, so don't be surprised if you lose three clubs on the go.

8. *Partner opens one of a suit.*

When partner opens with a suit, you should be pleased to have some values in that suit. But your enthusiasm should be contained temporarily for a variety of reasons.

1. If partner has opened with one club or one diamond, there is a chance that he has only a three-card suit and a bad one at that. Opposite

♠ A J 8 7
♡ K Q 5
♢ A 10 4
♣ 8 6 5

your Q 3 of clubs will be quite worthless.

2. Even if partner opens with a major suit, promising four, or in some systems, five, your honors may not be carrying full weight. Partner will have length in the suit, but it may lack quality. For instance

♠ 10 6 5 4 2
♡ A K 5
♢ K Q 5
♣ Q 2

Everyone would open one spade. If this is the case, Q 3 will not contribute very much to the hand.

The point of this is that when partner opens the bidding in a suit, it is more an expression of suit length than suit strength. Your honors may be working, but for the time being, you should be pleased rather than enthusiastic with them.

This also applies when partner rebids a new suit on a sequence such as:

Partner	You
1♣	1♡
1♠	

or

1♡	1♠
2♣	

On the first of these sequences,   1♣   1♡
                                        1♠

partner almost always has four. Also, there is no particular promise of high cards, so your evaluation of fitting high cards should
be similar to when partner opened the bidding in the suit.

On the second of these sequences, 1♡   1♠
                                      2♣

partner will usually have four, but may have five. If he does have
four clubs, they will probably be reasonable, or else he would
look elsewhere for a rebid.

♠ 10 7 6 5
♡ K 2
◊ A K J 5 4
♣ K 3

After 1◊   Pass   1♡   Pass
?

it would be reasonable to rebid one spade.

♠ K 3
♡ K 2
◊ A K J 5 4
♣ 10 7 6 5

After 1◊   Pass   1♡   Pass
?

it would be more descriptive to rebid one notrump than two clubs.
This implies that when opener bids a new suit at the two level,
you can upgrade fitting honors more than if opener had bid a new
suit at the one level.

9. *Partner opens and rebids his suit.*
Your first impression should be that fitting honors are quite valuable, and they will be. There are, however, three quite different situations and they should be evaluated differently.
1. You respond at the one level and partner rebids his suit.

1♡   Pass   1♠   Pass
2♡

On this sequence, partner has a six-card suit so your honors
will be quite useful. Nonetheless, partner's suit may be poor. Six
to the ten is a real, though minor, possibility.

2. You respond at the two level and partner rebids his suit.

1♡	Pass	2◇	Pass
2♡			

On this sequence, you should upgrade fitting heart honors, but not quite as much as after the prior auction. This is because your partner may have been forced by systemic constraints into rebidding a poorish suit.

For example, you open one heart on:

♠ K 8 7
♡ Q 10 8 6 5
◇ 3
♣ A K 9 7

If partner responds one spade, you would raise to two spades, or would rebid two clubs. Under no circumstances would you rebid two hearts.

If partner responded two diamonds, you would have no options. You couldn't rebid two notrump for a variety of reasons. Stiff diamond, not enough values. And you couldn't rebid three clubs either. The hand is at least an ace light for that. What's left is two hearts. You are not bidding two hearts so much because you have good hearts (you don't) but because other bids are worse.

3. The third sequence is really not a sequence, but rather a situation. It is when the opponents compete and partner voluntarily rebids his suit.

Typical auctions are:

1♡	Pass	1♠	2♣
2♡			

1♡	Pass	1♠	double
2♡			

1♡	Pass	1NT	2♣
2♡			

1♡	Pass	2♣	2◇
2♡			

On all of these sequences, partner had the option of passing. Instead, he chose to bid. The one thing which is clear here is that partner has a good suit. He may have extra values also, but these aren't as sure a thing as the suit quality.

Note that throughout the discussions, there have been occasional references to both the worth of a fitting card and its potential for fulfilling that worth. This is not a contradiction. On some sequences, you expect a card to have a certain value, and in the long run, it does achieve that value. However, that card is occasionally worthless, and occasionally worth more than you can imagine. In the long run, the card was worth what you expected it to be, but on any given hand, you could not tell what it was really worth. On some sequences however, you will find that your estimate is very frequently realized.

Compare these situations. You have:

$$\heartsuit \ K \ 3$$

1. You are the dealer. You hope the king is worth three points. Some of the time LHO has the A Q J and your king is worthless. Some of the time the A Q J is on your right and you get a trick. Some of the time your partner has an honor and your king combines. Add them all up and your king is a useful value. But as the dealer, you have no idea what that value will be.
2. When partner opens one heart, you will be pleased to have the K 3 and will rate it as more than three points. Perhaps eighty-five percent of the time it will be worth more than three points.
3. When partner opens one notrump, you will again like the K 3 of hearts, although not as much as when he opened one heart. After a one notrump opening, you would expect the heart king to be useful, say seventy percent of the time.
4. When LHO opens one heart, you will be discouraged about the king of hearts, but it may still prove important. Maybe twenty percent of the time.
5. And finally, getting back to where partner opens and then competitively rebids his suit, if you have the K 3, you will rate it highly, and you will realize that upwards of ninety-five percent of the time. This is an important concept to keep in mind. There will be times where you need to know exactly what a hand is worth now, rather than what it is worth in the long run.

10. *RHO opens with one of a suit.*

When this happens, you will experience good news and bad news. The bad news is that you will not be getting any length tricks in the suit they opened. The good news is that honors in opener's suit have the potential to be useful defensively or even offensively if your side declares.

Honors in other side suits go up in value, but only slightly. An opening bid in a suit does not promise as much in high cards as does one notrump so there is not as much reason to feel your side values are well placed. With the probability of fewer high cards on your right there is greater potential that LHO has honor cards over yours.

11. *RHO opens and LHO raises.*

Honors in side suits are treated about the same as before LHO raised. But honors in the opponents' suit go way downhill. They do not devaluate as much as when LHO opened and RHO raised, but the decline is still serious.

Most of what I said in part three of this section applies here, but there are one or two differences. The holding Q x x for example has the potential of being a defensive trick, which it always did. But if your side plays the hand, it may be sufficient to keep the opponents from tapping partner. RHO may have the A K x x and be unable to continue the suit after leading the king.

If your holding is better, say K x x or K J x, you have a good chance of taking a trick, but if partner has a stiff, the trick you take may be of little value. Nevertheless, a trick is a trick, so it need not be all bad.

12. *RHO opens one notrump.*

You should take the view that the honors you have are upgraded slightly in that they may take tricks, but you should not expect length tricks until such time that partner shows length in a suit. Note that your high cards take on more significance after an opening one notrump than after a sut bid by RHO. Even so, you should prefer to hear RHO open with a suit because your honors will have a better chance of reaching their maximum potential than if RHO starts with one notrump.

13. *Partner overcalls.*

Partner can overcall in a number of situations and according to the auction, your enthusiasm for fitting honors will range from mild to outrageous.

For example.

1. Partner can overcall at the one level after the opening bidder.

    1♣   1♠

2. Partner can overcall at the one level after opener's partner has responded.

    1♣   Pass   1♡   1♠

3. Partner can overcall at the two level on a number of sequences.

1♣	Pass	1♠	2♡
1♣	Pass	1NT	2♡
1♣	Pass	2♣	2♡
1♢	Pass	2♣	2♡

4. Partner can overcall at the three level on a variety of sequences.

1 ♠	Pass	2 ♡	3 ♣
1 ♠	Pass	2 ♠	3 ♣
		2 ♠ *	3 ♣
		(*weak)	

Obviously, the quality of partner's suit will vary from sequence to sequence and the vulnerability will be important as well.

When partner has a so-so suit, your honors will go up in value. But they won't go up as much as when partner has a good suit.

You can't always tell what kind of suit partner has, but you can always tell what his worst suit will be.

For example. No one vul.

Opener	Partner
1 ♣	1 ♠

Partner is likely to have a good suit, but there are some hands which would overcall with a suit as poor as 9 x x x.

> ♠ 9 8 7 6 3
> ♡ A Q 2
> ◊ 3
> ♣ A J 8 7

After a 1 ♣ opening, this hand would qualify for a 1 ♠ overcall. But only at the one level, and probably not vulnerable.

By comparison, with both sides vulnerable, if the auction started

Opener	You	Responder	Partner
1 ♠	Pass	2 ♣	?

Partner would not overcall with

> ♠ A 7
> ♡ K J 7 6 5
> ◊ K Q 10
> ♣ Q 4 2

but would overcall with

> ♠ 10 7 6 5
> ♡ K Q J 10 8 6
> ◊ A 2
> ♣ 3

Or, with no one vulnerable,

$$\spadesuit \ Q \ 10 \ 7 \ 6 \ 3$$
$$\heartsuit \ A \ K \ 2$$
$$\diamondsuit \ A \ 7 \ 6$$
$$\clubsuit \ 10 \ 2$$

You would expect partner to overcall two spades after

1 ◊	Pass	2 ◊	2 ♠

but not after

1 ◊	Pass	2 ♣	Pass

The reasons for all this are quite complex and I suggest you refer to my book on OVERCALLS for a complete discussion.

The point is that when you know the worst possible suit partner may have for his overcall, you will be able to determine

1. What is the guaranteed value of your fitting honors.
2. What is the potential value of your fitting honors.

If partner overcalls one spade, not vulnerable, and you have K 10 7 of spades, you have a lot of potential. But the K 10 7 of spades are not guaranteed. They should be worth something, and in the long run they will be worth a lot, but you may be disappointed now and then.

But if partner overcalls vulnerable after

1 ◊	Pass	2 ♣	2 ♠

then he must have a good suit and your K 10 7 will have a guaranteed worth as opposed to a potential worth.

The occasional poor suit notwithstanding, your partner will have a good suit far more often when overcalling than for any other action. And as a result, you will find fitting honors going up in value more than at any other time.

There is one last general area of hand evaluation which is in total contrast to those areas already discussed.

So far, all the combinations have been headed by some variety of honors.

But what happens when you have no honors in a suit? What if you have a stiff, or a small doubleton or perhaps three small? Is there anything about an apparently worthless holding which can give you cause to cheer. Or are small cards always a disappointment?

Let's take a look at each in turn.

You Have A Small Singleton.

The value of a small singleton is usually cut and dried. It is either good or bad. Seldom in-between. If partner bids the suit it is poor. If it is not in partner's suit, the presumption is you are looking at trump support so the stiff will be useful. If partner ends up playing notrump, your singleton will be poor if partner needs to play this suit.

Say you have

♠ 8
♡ Q 10 7 5
♢ K 6 4 2
♣ Q 9 6 3

LHO opens 1♠ and partner overcalls a 15- to 18-point 1NT. What is your hand worth?

Who knows? I would chance 2♣, asking for hearts. If partner has four hearts, my stiff spade may be significant. Opposite A 10 6 2 or Q 9 7 2, my stiff will be good. But opposite K Q 10 7 or A K J, it will have little value. If partner doesn't have four hearts, I'll try two no-trump, and the stiff spade will be of no value at all.

You Have Two Small.

When you have two small, your feelings are usually along neutral lines. If partner bids the suit, you have passive support. If partner needs to play this suit for tricks, your two small will be useful. If the opponents bid the suit, your doubleton will assure you have no more than two losers. When the opponents bid and raise a suit, two small is poor in that you have the worst possible number of cards, but it is good in that you have no wasted high cards. When the opponents bid and raise a suit, two small offers a curious side benefit. The opponents' bidding suggests partner has no honors in the suit. If so, you will have a doubleton facing a doubleton. This in itself is poor, but it means that whatever values you have will be useful. If partner has Q x or K x, these values may be worthless, but at least from *your* point of view, nothing was wasted.

You Have Three Small.

The real adventure in hand evaluation comes when you have *three* small. This combination is the most expressive of all holdings, and ranges in value from delightful to truly horrible.

Three small, by itself, tends to be less valuable than two small. But as soon as the bidding begins your estimate of it will change, and quickly.

Here are a few sample situations.

1. Partner bids one spade and you have 8 7 2. Immediately, your spades attain some minimal, but positive, value. At worst, you have a trump suit.
2. RHO opens one spade and you still have 8 7 2. This is the worst possible spade holding. Of all the common problems of evaluation, there is none where a holding so fully realizes its downside potential.
3. RHO opens one spade.

♠ 8 7 2
♡ A K J 7 6
♢ A K 8
♣ 9 2

You judge to overcall two hearts, correctly, but with some concern. Three small in the opponent's suit is so bad that some good players claim they will not overcall. Period. I don't adhere to this philosophy, and I don't believe they do either. But the fact is that three small is the cause for many large sets. Even this good hand can come to grief on a bad day.

The auction continues:

1♠   2♡   2♠

Suddenly those three small spades begin to sparkle. Partner is short, so you may hope for a minimum of heart tolerance. At this stage, those three small spades are beginning to look like an asset.

And it would be even better. Perhaps this is the auction

1♠   2♡   4♠   5♡
Pass   ?

All of a sudden, those three small spades become gold. Partner has one spade maximum and could have none. You will probably pass five hearts, but it could easily be right to continue. Partner could have

♠ 10
♡ Q 10 6 3
♢ Q 10 7 5 2
♣ A 8 3

and you're cold for six hearts. or

♠ —
♡ 8 5 4 3 2
♢ Q J 7 3
♣ A 8 6 3

which can produce seven hearts.

When the auction tells you partner is short in your three small suit, and partner's raise tells you he likes your suit, you have hit a gold mine. If partner is short, then he won't have wasted high cards which means that whatever high cards he does have will be working for you.

Here is a curious extension of this. You have the following two fine hands.

♠ 8 6 2	♠ K 8 2
♡ 10 5 4 3	♡ 10 5 4 3
◊ 9 6 3	◊ 9 6 3
♣ 8 5 2	♣ 8 5 2

The auction goes

LHO	Partner		
1♠	2♡	3♠	Pass
Pass	Double	Pass	4♡

Partner's sequence shows in order:

1. Good hearts
2. Support for all suits.

He probably has a 1-6-3-3 hand, or something approximating it. Your hand, aside from its four hearts, will be a disappointment. However, the second hand will be a bigger disappointment than the first.

The opponents' auction promises around twenty-one high card points, so your side has around nineteen. In the first hand, your partner has those nineteen and they are all working. On the second hand, he has sixteen points, all working. He was hoping you would have a useful three or four points. You don't have them. Your only value, the spade king, is not working. Partner would far have preferred a couple of minor suit jacks to the spade king.

I would expect you to go down one more trick on the second hand than on the first hand, even though both hands have the same net worth.

Chapter III

ELASTIC EVALUATION –
UPGRADING AND DOWNGRADING YOUR HAND

In the rest of this book, I will be looking at many hands. In each case there will be a number of auctions. Some of the time it will be up to you to make a decision. Sometimes not. Rather than what to do, the important question will be, how do you feel about the hand at this point in the auction. Has it gotten better? Has it worsened? Is it the same as always?

On those occasions where you do need to make a decision, I will look into what you should do and why. There are a few worthwhile guidelines which I will introduce and discuss.

You are the dealer.

♠ K 8 6 2
♡ K 10 2
◇ 8 5
♣ J 8 5 2

At this stage, you have a nothing hand worth perhaps eight points. Small plusses are that your four card suits have honors and you have the ten of hearts with the king. Hands with secondary cards are usually hard to define early. Since this is hardly an opening bid you should pass and wait to see how it develops. Who knows? Perhaps you have a good hand. Digressing a moment, I held this hand recently.

♠ K J 7 3
♡ K J 5
◇ K J 4
♣ K Q 3

I opened one notrump and it went double by LHO. Five down. Minus 900. The point is that my kings and jacks found no combining values in dummy so totally failed to fulfill their potential. It is the same with the hand being discussed above. By itself, it is worthless. Will it ripen? The auction will tell.

♠ K 8 6 2
♡ K 10 2
◇ 8 5
♣ J 8 5 2

Partner	RHO	You
1♠	Pass	?

The king of spades takes on a nice lustre and the fourth trump comes into its own quite nicely. The difference between three and four trumps is significant. Perhaps it translates into a point. Also, now that a fit has been established, the doubleton diamond has tentative value.

The heart king goes up in value because with partner's announced strength, there is a better than a priori chance that he has the ace.

This hand should raise to two spades. What is it worth? I would say 10+ points arrived at thusly.

♠ K 8 6 2	3 plus 1 for the fitting honor plus 1 for the fourth trump.
♡ K 10 2	3 plus ½ for the fitting ten spot.
◇ 8 5	1
♣ J 8 5 2	¾ Unclear. Jacks are hard to evaluate until you get specific information.

By my evaluation, I should bid more than two spades, but that would be pushing it a bit. Ten and a half points represents the maximum potential and something may happen to some of my "extra" values. However, until you learn otherwise, it can't hurt to be optimistic.

♠ K 8 6 2
♡ K 10 2
◇ 8 5
♣ J 8 5 2

Partner	RHO	You	LHO
1 ♠	Pass	2 ♠	Pass
3 ♡			

With both kings now achieving maximum promotion, you should bid game and expect it to be cold. Note that your doubleton diamond diminishes a little as does your jack of clubs. However, the increased value of the heart king is far greater than the decrease in value of your minor suit holdings.

♠ K 8 6 2
♡ K 10 2
◇ 8 5
♣ J 8 5 2

Partner	RHO	You	LHO
1 ♠	Pass	2 ♠	Pass
3 ◇			

The value now takes on a hypothetical quality. Your spade holding is excellent, but your heart holding does not increase any after the three diamond bid. The doubleton diamond, however, takes on additional value for two reasons. First, even though you haven't a fitting honor, your dou-

38

bleton guarantees that later losers in the suit can be ruffed. Secondly, you have a fourth trump, so even if the defense leads them, the defense won't be nearly as effective as if you had three trumps.

An additional point is that your doubleton diamond is facing length. Partner would not make a game try in a short suit, so you know you won't have matching doubletons.

The sum of this is that you should bid four spades. But don't be nearly as confident as when partner's game try was three hearts. If you choose three spades only, I would think it conservative, but it could work.

♠ K 8 6 2
♡ K 10 2
♢ 8 5
♣ J 8 5 2

Partner	RHO	You	LHO
1♠	Pass	2♠	Pass
3♢	Pass	3♠	Pass
4♡			

In the event that you choose three spades and partner tries again, you have to make yet another decision. But it is not like any of the previous decisions. Partner's three diamond bid was, for the moment, a game try. The four heart bid, however, commits you to game and is expressing interest in slam.

What now?

The first thing is to determine what the hand is worth. And the answer is, a lot.

The spades as usual are worth quite a bit.

The heart king now assumes near maximum value.

The diamond doubleton remains valuable.

Only the club jack seems to have lost its potential, and considering the improvement elsewhere, the loss of one point is nothing.

PRINCIPLE – THE BOX

Before deciding what to do with the actual hand, I want to express a principle which can frequently be used when making decisions in constructive sequences. For want of a name, I call it the BOX principle, or just BOX. It works this way.

Often during the bidding, you will have made a limited bid showing a specific range of values.

For example.

	Partner		You	
			1NT = 15-17	
	1♣	Pass	2NT = 13-14	
	1♣	Pass	2♣ = 6-10	
			1♣	
Pass	1♡	Pass	2♡ = 12-15	
	1♡	Pass	Pass = 0-5	

By comparison, these bids are all undefined in that your range is not limited.

	Partner		You	
			1♣	
Pass	1♡	Pass	1♠	12-18
	1◇	Pass	1♡	6-20
	1♠	Double		11-23
	1◇	2♣		9-17
			2♣	
Pass	2◇	Pass	2♠	23-36
	1♠	Pass	2♣	10-20

On these sequences where you have defined your hand, it is said to be in a certain box. An opening 1NT showing 15 to 17 goes into the category or box of hands showing 15-17 points, no singletons, etc. No matter what happens later, partner will expect you to have that 15-17 points. As the auction proceeds, you may be able to more closely define your hand. In the example auction I've been discussing, 1♠-Pass-2♠, you have put your hand in the 6-10 point box with three or more spades.

When the auction continued,

1♠	Pass	2♠	Pass
3◇	Pass	3♠	

you redefined your hand as 6-8 points with spade support. At each stage of the auction, your hand was "boxed." And, whatever the box, that is what partner is going to think you have.

Now, when you have reached a stage of the auction where your hand has been boxed, and partner asks you a question, you answer his question within this framework, *i.e.*, given the box my hand is in, is my hand maximum or minimum?

Back to the hand

$$\spadesuit \text{ K 8 6 2}$$
$$\heartsuit \text{ K 10 2}$$
$$\diamondsuit \text{ 8 5}$$
$$\clubsuit \text{ J 8 5 2}$$

Partner			
1 ♠	Pass	2 ♠	Pass
3 ◊	Pass	3 ♠	Pass
4 ♡	Pass	?	

At this stage, you are considering whether to accept partner's slam try in light of your hand being in the 6-8 point box rather than the original 6-10 point box shown by the raise to two spades. In this context, your hand is enormous. After your third re-evaluation of the auction, your hand is worth around ten or eleven points. Partner wants to know if you have a useful eight. If you were to jump to six spades, it would be a fair expression of value. If you can't stand this, then bid at least five spades. The one thing you should not worry about is clubs. Partner is interested in a slam and you have two crucial kings. How can partner be missing both of these cards and also have two club losers?

I would guess partner has something like this.

$$\spadesuit \text{ A Q 10 7 4 3}$$
$$\heartsuit \text{ A Q 3}$$
$$\diamondsuit \text{ A Q 6 3}$$
$$\clubsuit \text{ —}$$

or

$$\spadesuit \text{ A Q J 7 3}$$
$$\heartsuit \text{ A Q 3}$$
$$\diamondsuit \text{ A K J 4}$$
$$\clubsuit \text{ 6}$$

This box principle comes up quite frequently. I will be referring to it constantly in later chapters.

Here are two more hands showing the box principle at work.

No one vulnerable.   *Hand A*

$$\spadesuit \text{ J 9 8 7 5}$$
$$\heartsuit \text{ 8 7 3}$$
$$\diamondsuit \text{ Q 5 4}$$
$$\clubsuit \text{ 10 6}$$

Partner	RHO	You
1 ◊	Pass	Pass

At this stage, there is very little to like about your hand. The one thing which is clear cut is that you should pass. In your favor at least is that you do have trump support. Compared with

Hand B

♠ J 9 8 7 6 3
♡ J 10 5 4
◇ —
♣ 8 6 2

you do not have to worry that one diamond is a horrible contract and also that you might have a game in spades or hearts. Pass would still be best because with Hand B the dangers of bidding would outweigh the dangers of passing. Unfortunately when passing is wrong, it is frightfully wrong. Likewise for bidding.

No one vulnerable.

Partner	RHO	You	LHO
1 ◇	Pass	Pass	1 ♡
Double	Pass	?	

♠ J 9 8 7 5
♡ 8 7 3
◇ Q 5 4
♣ 10 6

What was originally a terrible hand suddenly has acquired a redeeming feature. Actually, a number of them. Your queen and jack can be counted on and you have a five card suit where partner would most like you to have it, *i.e.*, spades. Your correct bid here is one spade, but you should feel that you have a maximum for this. Remember, your pass to one diamond put your hand in the 0-5 point box, and in spite of this, partner wants to hear from you. Within this 0-5 point range, you have just average high cards, but you have them where they will count for something and you have a five card suit.

No one vulnerable.

♠ J 9 8 7 5
♡ 8 7 3
◇ Q 5 4
♣ 10 6

Partner	RHO	You	LHO
1 ◇	Pass	Pass	1 ♡
Double	Pass	1 ♠	Pass
2 ♡	Pass		

The box gets smaller and smaller, and your hand gets better and better. When you passed one diamond, you showed 0-5. When you bid one spade, you showed 0-3. With a decent four or five, you would have bid more than one spade.

Partner	RHO	You	LHO
1◊	Pass	Pass	1♡
Double	Pass	?	

♠ K J 8 7 5
♡ 8 5 3
◊ 10 6 4
♣ 8 2

You would, or should, jump to two spades.

Therefore, having bid only one spade, you have boxed your hand in the 0-3 range. Partner is still interested in a game. If he is willing to try for game knowing you have a bad hand, you must let him know you have a maximum hand. Jump to three spades.

You may wonder how you can have a game when partner failed to open with a strong two bid. Don't. You will go crazy trying to construct hands. Instead, simply accept the fact that even after two denial bids by you, partner is still trying. Let him do the worrying. If you get to four spades and go down, it will be because things broke poorly, or because partner didn't have his values. Neither case should concern you. You had your values. If you must know what partner had, I will offer these possibilities.

♠ A Q 6 3
♡ J 2
◊ A J 10 2
♣ A K J

Four spades will be on a finesse.

♠ A K 10 2
♡ 3
◊ K J 10 3
♣ A Q J 7

Not cold, but very playable.

Vul vs. not.

You	LHO	Partner	RHO
1♣	Pass	1♠	Pass
2♣	Pass	3♣ *	Pass
?		(*forcing)	

♠ K 10 4 2
♡ K 5 3
◊ 7 3
♣ K Q J 4

Having boxed your hand at 12-15, the question is whether you have a maximum. You do have good trumps, your clubs are working, and your heart king is prime. Against this, you have poorish shape and no aces. Three spades is enough.

You	LHO	Partner	RHO
1♣	Pass	1♠	Pass
2♠	Pass	3♣ *	Pass
3♠	Pass	4◊	Pass
?		(*forcing)	

♠ K 10 4 2
♡ K 5 3
◊ 7 3
♣ K Q J 4

The hand remains a good minimum. Sufficient to bid four spades. Your black suit holdings are excellent but for slam purposes, you have no help in diamonds and your heart king will probably be of tactical use only.

You	LHO	Partner	RHO
1♣	Pass	1♠	Pass
2♠	Pass	3♣ *	Pass
3♠	Pass	4◊	Pass
4♠	Pass	5♡	Pass
?		(*forcing)	

♠ K 10 4 2
♡ K 5 3
◊ 7 3
♣ K Q J 4

Finally. You have denied a maximum hand and you have denied a good hand and partner is still looking. Partner knows you are minimum and wants to know if your minimum is working. It is. When partner bid one spade, it turned your spades into a good holding. When partner bid three clubs, your clubs became prime values. These clubs are far more valuable when not facing a stiff or doubleton. Partner's club bid was music. When partner bid four diamonds, your hand did not change much. The doubleton is not worth too much on this sequence because four diamonds does not imply length but rather a control. Compare with

1♠	Pass	2♣	Pass
3♣			

On this sequence, 3♣ shows a suit so if responder has a small doubleton, it will go up a bit in value.

When partner cuebids four diamonds, the only plus for you is that partner is showing slammish strength which means four spades should be cold. The slight minus to four diamonds is that partner seems worried about hearts. If the defense leads hearts, your heart king may or may not be worthwhile.

But now, when partner cuebids five hearts, your heart king comes into its own and your minimum has suddenly started working overtime. The only thing you might prefer is to have the spade jack instead of the club jack.

What you should bid is unclear. What is clearer is that your hand has been boxed at 12-13 and in fact it is closer to 15 or 16.

If partner has

♠ A Q 8 3
♡ A 9 5
◇ A 8 7
♣ A 6 4

six spades is cold on three-two trumps and may survive some four-one breaks.

If partner has

♠ A Q 8 5 3
♡ A 7
◇ A 2
♣ A 7 6 2

the winning spot is seven clubs.

I'm not sure how to get to seven clubs on the second hand. Perhaps if I bid six clubs, partner will know to bid seven. What I do know though, is that I am getting to some slam. I am not bidding five spades over five hearts. The box principle says I have much more than my last bid shows. Partner has invited, and I have extras. I accept.

Note that the twelve point hand became worth upwards of sixteen. This is what happens when you have an auction such that each of your high cards becomes of known value. By comparison.

Partner	RHO	You	LHO
1♠	Pass	2♣	Pass
3◇	Pass	4♠	Pass
5♡	Pass	?	

You

- ♠ 8 7 6 2
- ♡ 8 6 2
- ◊ J 5 4 3
- ♣ A K

You went to four spades based on general values. As far as slam goes though you have little of clear value. Unless partner is specifically looking for club control, your hand is worth very little. Partner may have

- ♠ A Q 10 5 3
- ♡ A Q 2
- ◊ A K 10 2
- ♣ 7

Losers all over.

Partner	RHO	You	LHO
—	—	1 ♣	Pass
1 ♠	Pass	2 ♠	Pass
3 ◊	Pass	4 ♠	Pass
5 ♡	Pass	?	

You

- ♠ A Q J 2
- ♡ 8 5 4
- ◊ Q 8 3
- ♣ K Q J

Once again, your values caused you to bid four spades. But you did so because of general strength rather than fit. Partner's sequence has actually not done a thing for your hand. True, you have good spades, but the jack may be redundant. Your heart holding can't be worse. Your diamond holding has some value now, but you can't tell if it is useful or terrific. And your club holding. What is it worth? If, as the bidding suggests, partner is short, then your clubs may provide a couple of discards, but those discards may come too late, or they may not even be worthwhile discards. This fifteen-point hand has a terrible disposition of high cards. With its working values being minimal, it may be worth less than half of its face value.

SHELL POINTS

Cards which are known to be working and hence have guaranteed value are sometimes described as the "shell."
For instance

```
♠ A 8 4 2
♡ A 6 5
◇ A 6 2
♣ A 8 3
```

The aces are probably working, hence each is part of the shell. Note there is no auction. Aces are good cards except under unusual circumstances.

Partner	RHO	You	LHO
1 ◇	Pass	1 ♠	Pass
2 ♣	Pass	?	

You

```
♠ K Q 5 4 2
♡ Q 10 8
◇ 5 4
♣ 10 6 3
```

For partner's purpose, none of your values can be guaranteed, so your shell is worthless. You should pass two clubs and feel that you may be providing a totally worthless hand.

Partner		You	
1 ◇	Pass	1 ♠	Pass
2 ♣	Pass	?	

You

```
♠ 8 6 5 4 2
♡ 10 6 3
◇ K 2
♣ K J 3
```

Pass again. But with all your minor cards working, you have a seven point shell. Another club, and you would raise.

Partner	RHO	You	LHO
1 ♠	Pass	2 ◇	Pass
2 ♡	Pass	3 ♣	Pass
3 ♡	Pass	3NT	Pass
4 ♡	Pass	Pass	Pass

You

♠ Q
♡ J 3
◇ K Q 10 9 7
♣ K Q J 6 4

Opposite partner's auction, you have only three points, the spade queen and the heart jack, working toward your shell. Your lack of a third trump somewhat erodes this shell, so it is worth only three points in principle. Partner will not like this dummy.

Partner	RHO	You	LHO
Pass	Pass	1 ♠	Pass
4 ♣ *	Pass		

*singleton with trump support (see Chapter V)

♠ A K 8 6 3
♡ K 2
◇ K 2
♣ 8 6 5 4

Your shell is probably thirteen points, and the four little clubs have value also because three of them can be ruffed. If partner can provide

♠ 10 9 5 4 3
♡ A 8 7
◇ A 10 6 2
♣ 7

an eight point shell, or

♠ Q 10 7 2
♡ A 8 6 5
◇ A 9 5 4
♣ 2

a ten point shell, we have a slam.

Note that when you describe "shell" points, there is no need to inflate them. By definition, they are worth much more than their face value. Six shell points are usually more valuable than 15 or 20 non-shell points.

This provides a very useful guideline. Whenever you have limited your hand, if you have all shell points, you have a maximum. If your points are, or may be, non-shell, then you may have a minimum.

One last point.

Shell points are points which are of guaranteed value. But what is guaranteed for one contract may not be guaranteed for another.

Partner	RHO	You	LHO
1♣	Pass	1♠	Pass
2♦	Pass	?	

You

♠ Q J 10 7 5
♡ 3
◊ Q J 10 4 2
♣ K 6

With partner raising spades, you have an excellent hand. It is hard to count your shell points, but everything you have looks like it can be translated into tricks. This is a good hand and you would go to four spades. BUT

Partner	RHO	You	LHO
1♣	Pass	1♠	Pass
2♣	Pass	?	

You

♠ Q J 10 7 5
♡ 3
◊ Q J 10 4 2
♣ K 6

With partner rebidding clubs, you have little of sure value to offer partner. You can count on the club king, but the queens and jacks are no bargain. You could procede with two diamonds, but gingerly.

Distribution doesn't exactly qualify for shell points, but it is obvious that some singletons, for example, are better than others. Say partner opens one spade and RHO overcalls two clubs. You can choose from either of these hands.

♠ K J 8 7   ♠ K J 8 7
♡ Q 10 4 3 2   ♡ Q 10 4 3 2
◊ 9 7 3   ◊ 2
♣ 2   ♣ 9 7 3

You would certainly prefer the first hand. RHO has club strength so the chances are lessened that your partner has something wasted. In the second hand your three small clubs offer the possibility of two or three losers. Another two hands.

Partner	RHO	You	LHO
1♠	Pass	3♠	Pass
4◊	Pass	4♡	Pass
5♣	Pass	?	

Partner is asking about the club suit.

♠ K J 8 7 4	♠ K J 8 7 4
♡ A K 10 8	♡ A K 10 8
◇ 3	◇ 8 7 5
♣ 8 7 5	♣ 3

You have a club control in the second hand but not the first.

Opposite partner's hand, it is clear that all singletons are not the same.

♠ A Q 10 6 3
♡ 4
◇ A K Q J
♣ 10 9 4

You do not predicate all decisions on shell points. Sometimes you don't have any, but your hand is so good generally speaking that you proceed anyway. For instance, after

1 ♠	Pass	2 ♠	Pass
3 ♠	Pass	?	

you would continue to four spades with

♠ 8 7 6 5
♡ K 5 4
◇ K 10 4
♣ K J 3

In spite of no shell points, you would go on general principles.

But you would pass with

♠ K 8 6 5
♡ Q J 4
◇ 4 2
♣ 8 6 3 2

This hand has good spades, but is minimum otherwise.

However, change the auction to

1 ♠	Pass	2 ♠	Pass
3 ♡	Pass	?	

♠ K 8 6 5
♡ Q J 4
◇ 4 2
♣ 8 6 3 2

and you have six shell points plus a possibly useful doubleton. You would bid four spades and feel that these six shell points will make this a claimer.

50

By comparison, when the auction went

1♠	Pass	2♠	Pass
3♠	Pass	4♠	

and you had

> ♠ 8 7 6 5
> ♡ K 5 4
> ◇ K 10 4
> ♣ K J 3

You could not feel quite as confident, ten points notwithstanding.

LHO	Partner	RHO	You
1◇	1NT*	Pass	?
	(*15-18)		

> ♠ Q 8 7
> ♡ 8 2
> ◇ Q 8 6 5 4
> ♣ K J 8

With LHO bidding diamonds, there is the likelihood that your diamond length will not be of value. If opener has four, or even five diamonds, it will be either difficult or impossible to get more than your high card tricks out of the diamond suit.

This means that your hand probably offers high card help only. This hand is worth only eight points and not particularly good ones at that. Pass.

There is another danger. Partner chose to overcall one notrump rather than double. There is a moderate chance that he is weak in hearts. If so, a heart lead could be effective. On those occasions, RHO will usually find this lead. Remember, RHO has only a stiff or doubleton diamond so he may have length elsewhere. Probably it will be in hearts.

LHO	Partner	RHO	You
1♡	1NT	Pass	?

> ♠ Q 8 7
> ♡ 8 2
> ◇ Q 8 6 5 4
> ♣ K J 8

With LHO opening one heart instead of one diamond, you can be more optimistic. Now there is no need to fear the heart suit since partner will have them stopped. And your diamond length rates to be an asset, where before it was not. Raise to two notrump.

Here is a possible hand for partner to have.

♠ Q 8 7
♡ 8 2
◊ Q 8 6 5 4
♣ K J 8
□
♠ K J 4
♡ K J 3
◊ K J 3
♣ A 9 6 2

If RHO has opened one heart, the chances are that he has the A Q of hearts. Plus diamonds rate to divide in normal 3-2 fashion.

If RHO opens one diamond, your expectations are far less because diamonds no longer rate to break, and there is less expectation that RHO has both heart honors. It is not easy to determine how many tricks these hands are worth, but it is easy to see that they are worth more when RHO opens with one heart.

Note that when the auction goes 1♡-1NT, your partner implies no interest in spades, so he rates to have a fit for clubs or diamonds. On this hand, you can hope for a diamond fit. By comparison,

LHO	Partner	RHO	You
1♡	1NT	Pass	?

♠ Q 8 6 5 4
♡ 8 2
◊ K J 8
♣ Q 8 7

Your high cards have the usual value associated with being opposite a one notrump opener. The important point of this hand is that the spades may be less valuable than either clubs or diamonds. Partner will often overcall one notrump with four clubs A K x x, but would hesitate to do so with A K x x of spades. This means that as far as notrump goes, you won't be able to realize length tricks as often as if your long suit were a minor.

What to do with this hand is another question. If available, I would transfer and then bid two notrump. If transfers are not available, you will have to do some guessing. I would choose an invitational sequence of some sort, probably two clubs (Stayman) followed by two spades.

Notice that on all of these invitational sequences, your decisions are based on general values rather than shell values. Almost always, shell values come in to play on suit oriented sequences rather than notrump sequences. The times shell values become useful in notrump sequences are when you need to take your nine tricks fast.

LHO	Partner	RHO	You
1♠	2♣	2♠	?

♠ A 9 7
♡ K Q 4
◊ K J 9 6 5
♣ 10 2

You have a good hand, but as far as three notrump goes, there are no guarantees. The opponents will lead spades knocking out your ace. You will need eight more tricks in a hurry and if partner hasn't the right cards, you will be in trouble. Does partner have

♠ 10 2	or	♠ 7
♡ A 9		♡ 8 5
◊ Q 10 4		◊ A 10 4
♣ K Q J 9 7 5		♣ A Q J 8 5 4 3

One hand offers no play for three notrump and the second hand requires a finesse. Your red suit honors turn out to be of little use. The only shell card your hand offers is the ace of spades. Your red cards have potential, but they do not always have time to live up to it.

LHO	Partner	RHO	You
1♠	2♣	2♠	?

♠ J 10 6 3
♡ A 2
◊ A 8 6 5 4
♣ Q 8

This quick trick hand is overflowing with shell points. It looks like only ten shell points, but when you consider that partner has overcalled at the two level, he should have a good suit. This means you can raise the club queen a bit since it should be both a winner and it should help establish *fast* length tricks. Try three notrump.

No one vulnerable.

LHO	Partner	RHO	You
—	1♡	Pass	1♠
Pass	2♠	Pass	?

♠ K Q 6 5 4 2
♡ K Q
◊ 3 2
♣ A Q 6

Game should be cold and slam is possible. If partner's shell consists of three aces, you may have thirteen tricks.

Since this is a possible holding and since there is room to explore for it, it is reasonable to make a try. Start with three clubs.

As long as you can make your slam try without getting beyond your safety level, you should do so.

The shell principle won't help you decide what to bid, but it will help you decide when to bid. On this hand, the shell principle says slam is possible. And for the moment, the safety principle says you can make a slam try.

Both vulnerable.

LHO	Partner	RHO	You
—	—	—	1 ♠
2 ♡	4 ♠	Pass	?

♠ A Q 10 7 5
♡ Q 2
◊ 3
♣ A K Q J 9

Here, the shell principle says slam is possible. But the safety principle says it is far too dangerous to look for it.

True, partner could have

♠ K x x x
♡ x
◊ A x x x x x
♣ x x

or some such, but he is far more likely to have a hand like

♠ K x x x x
♡ x x
◊ K J x x
♣ x

When your slam try jeopardizes getting a plus score, give it up unless you have very, very strong expectations that partner can have the right hand.

Vul vs. not.

LHO	Partner	RHO	You
—	—	—	Pass
Pass	Pass	1 ♣	1 ♡
Pass	2 ♣	Pass	2 ♡
Pass	3 ♡	Pass	?

♠ 8 2
♡ K 10 8 6 5
◇ K 3
♣ A 9 4 2

The box principle works quite well here. In spite of his original pass, partner still wants to try for game. He knows you couldn't open the bidding. He heard you make a minimum rebid. He still thinks game is possible.

Should you bid it?

Yes. When you passed, you boxed your hand at less than thirteen points. When you signed off at two hearts you showed nothing extra.

Partner is asking whether, in light of your early bids, you have a maximum? And you do.

You have excellent high cards. Nearly an opening bid. Your kings are behind the opening bidder. Your shape is good. All in all, nothing but pluses.

Note that were you not a passed hand, you would reject the invitation.

Chapter IV

WARNING SIGNS

1. *Short compact suits.*

```
♠ 8 2
♡ J 5 4
◇ A Q J 10 5
♣ Q 6 4
```

Hands with stubby suits and soft outside cards are somewhat one dimensional. As dealer, you would pass. With no contribution from partner, you would overcall one diamond, auction permitting, and you might balance. But otherwise this hand will pass throughout. With most of the value concentrated in diamonds, you are assured of at least four winners, but you have little side potential. You will need a lot of fitting cards from partner to get this hand going. That ten of diamonds is nice, but the suit already is good enough in general that the ten would offer more potential if it were in hearts or clubs.

One of the problems with hands like this is that if you bid your diamonds and partner raises, your hand doesn't go up much in value. Your suit is so good that trump support doesn't improve the value of the suit. Compare with trump suits like Q 10 x x x which get raised. Q 10 x x x is a soft holding, but when partner raises, you can hope for as many as four or even five tricks.

When you start with A Q J 10 5, and partner raises, you have expectations of five tricks, but since you were already sure of four, the net isn't that much.

What you are experiencing here is duplication of values. It comes in many shapes and forms. In this instance, the duplication is in the form of excess trump value, sometimes known as "trump rich."

There are many kinds of duplication and I will look at a few of the more common. The basic idea is that on those occasions where you can tell that there is duplication, you will be able to make some appropriate adjustment in your evaluation.

2. *Excess trumps*

When you have a good suit and it gets raised, your hand does not go up as much in value as when you have a bad trump suit which gets raised. Typical examples include

A K Q 9 7

A Q J 10 9

A K Q J 10

K Q J 10 9

etc.

You open the bidding and partner raises. How good is this for you?

It is good insofar as you have found a fit, but it is not so good from other points of view. First, partner is less likely to have a trump honor, and in some cases, he can't have one, so his high cards will be in other suits where they may or may not be of value. Or, if his values are in trumps, then you will have what is known as duplication, or being trump rich. Trump suits like these

A 8 7 6 2

□

K Q J 9 3

It would be almost as good not to have the queen and jack. It would certainly be better to put them elsewhere.

A Q J 10 9

□

K 8 6 4

The jack is unnecessary and the queen possibly unnecessary.

3. *Blocked suits*

9 8 7 6

□

A K Q J 10

The jack and ten are not needed, and the queen may not be needed. This is like the previous example but is an added minus, the suit does not afford two-way communication. You can enter the South hand easily enough, but you can't enter the North hand. It would be so much better to have the suit arranged, say

K J 9 7

□

A Q 10 8 6

which would allow convenient back and forth communication.

This trump duplication can be seen from both sides of the table.

Partner	You
1♠	2♠
3♠	?

♠ K Q J 10 8
♡ 8 5 4
◊ 9 6 5
♣ 8 3

Perhaps you should continue on the basis of your good trumps, but I doubt it.

♠ K 9 8 6 5
♡ Q J 5
♣ 10 9 4
♣ 7 2

With almost equivalent trumps and potentially useful side cards, you could continue to four spades. Compare these dummies opposite this hand partner might hold.

Hand A	Hand B
♠ K Q J 10 9	♠ K 9 8 6 5
♡ 8 5 4	♡ Q J 5
◊ 9 6 5	◊ 10 9 4
♣ 8 3	♣ 7 2

Partner

♠ A 7 4 3 2
♡ K 9
◊ K Q 3
♣ A Q 4

Hand A as dummy could lose five tricks, although that would take a little bad luck.

Hand B though is just about cold for four spades. And it may succeed even against a bad trump break.

When you have a solid suit and partner raises, you can't judge the hand because you don't have a clue as to where partner's values really are. Here are some typical examples.

You	Partner
1♠	2♠

♠ A K Q J 10 7
♡ K Q
◊ 8 7
♣ Q 5 4

At this point in the auction, you do not know whether your maximum is two spades or five spades. You will either go to four spades, or perhaps make a game try, but whatever the auction, you won't be sure until you see dummy.

You	Partner
1♠	2♠

♠ Q 10 8 6 5 4
♡ 3
◊ A 5
♣ A Q J 5

Here, your hand has gone up immensely in value because of the improvement in trumps. Whatever partner has in spades will be useful, and this raise suggests he has an honor.

4. *Wasted honors*

Other forms of duplication include matching short suits with a concentration of high cards

A J	K Q 10	K 9	K Q J
K Q	A J 4	Q J	A 4

Sometimes you can tell this exists. Usually the opponents will have bid, or bid and raised a suit. You have A J of clubs.

LHO	Partner	RHO	You
1♣	Pass	2♣	2♡
Pass	2NT	Pass	?

You have A Q of hearts

LHO	Partner	RHO	You
1♡	1NT	2♡	?

You have Q 8 of hearts.

LHO	Partner	RHO	You
1◊	Pass	1♡	2♣
2♡	2NT	Pass	?

Now you should feel that the queen of hearts is almost a minus value. Unless partner has some secondary strength to go with his stopper, your heart queen will be compromised at trick one. Too bad you couldn't play it from your side.

5. *Duplicated shape*

The last form of duplication quite simply occurs when your hand and dummy's have the same shape.

♠ A K 8 6 5
♡ K 5 4
◇ K 2
♣ J 8 3

♠ Q J 9 4 2
♡ A 8 3
◇ Q 5
♣ A 7 4

Terrible. Wasted values in trumps and matching distribution. Three notrump anyone? If either hand had a different doubleton, four spades would be cold.

♠ K 8 7 6
♡ 8 5 4
◇ K J 7 6
♣ A 2

♠ Q J 9 5 4
♡ J 6 2
◇ A Q
♣ K Q 9

Same problem, sort of. Duplication in hearts. This time you can get rid of a loser if given time, but not if the opponents get after them.

In general, any time you have matching length in just one suit, that can be potentially bad. Three opposite three, two opposite two, singleton opposite singleton.

Some of the time, you can tell. Sometimes you can't. When the opponents are silent, it is almost impossible to know when a given suit lies poorly for you. But when the opponents get into the auction, you can frequently tell whether you have matching lengths in an opponent's suit.

For instance, you have three hearts.

LHO	Partner	RHO	You
1♡	1♠	1NT	Pass
2♣	Pass	2♡	?

Partner has three hearts also.

1♡	Pass	2♡	2♠
3♡	Pass	Pass	

Partner has two or one hearts.

1♡	Pass	2♡	2♠
Pass	Pass	3♡	

Partner has one heart.

LHO	Partner	RHO	You
—	—	1♡	1♠
Double*	2♠	Pass	
(*Negative)			

Partner has three or four hearts. LHO would have raised hearts if possible.

Or, you have two hearts.

LHO	Partner	RHO	You
1♡	Double	3♡	

Partner rates to have two hearts.

2♡*	3♣	3♡	
(* weak two bid)			

Partner rates to have a doubleton heart.

	1♠	2♡	2♠
3♡	3♠	4♡	

Unclear.

1♣	Double	1♢	Pass
1♡	1♠	2♡	

Partner has three hearts.

Or, you can have a stiff heart.

LHO	Partner	RHO	You
3♡	4♠	5♡	

It is possible for partner to have a stiff also.

Not vul. vs. vul.

Pass	1♠	2♡	3♠
4♡	4♠	5♡	

Again, partner may have a stiff.

The point of this is that when you can accurately judge that you and partner have matching length in the dangerous suit, it may be bad news. With three opposite three, you are exposed to the maximum number of losers. If you are two opposite two, you and partner may both have added something for a doubleton when you should have been subtracting. And if you both have singletons, each party may have regarded it as an asset when it was not.

The ability to discern duplication of any sort is useful, but it should not be overdone. For instance.

RHO	You	LHO	Partner
1♡	1♠	Pass	3♠
Pass	4♠		

♠ K Q 8 7 5
♡ K 6 4
◇ A Q 9 7
♣ J

Even if you could tell for sure that your partner had three small hearts, you would go on to four spades because your values compensate for the flaw.

RHO	You	LHO	Partner
1♠	2♡	2♠	3♡

♠ Q 7
♡ K J 9 7 6 5
◇ K Q
♣ Q 8 7

You shouldn't go on to four hearts anyway, but realizing that you have likely got two opposite two in spades plus the wasted queen, you should pass.

RHO	You	LHO	Partner
1♡	1♠	Double*	3♠
		(*Negative)	

♠ Q 10 8 7 5
♡ A 5 4
◇ K Q 8 7
♣ Q

Assuming three spades is forward going, you would tend to reject the invitation. LHO has short hearts so his heart lead will be an effective defense. You probably have enough to make four spades if left to your own devices, but here you are at the mercy of tempo. It's their lead, not yours.

Both vul. —————————

LHO	Partner	RHO	You
3 ♡	4 ♠	5 ♡	?

♠ Q J 8 3
♡ 3
♢ Q 7 6 5
♣ Q 7 6 4

I suppose I would go ahead and bid five spades. But I would not look at all fondly at the stiff heart. Partner probably has one too. If so, he can have a fine 6-1-3-3 for example and it will be hard for him to avoid any minor suit losers. Also, we may be experiencing some trump duplication although I am not going to apologize for the ones I have. There is one good thing about being trump rich. When the bidding gets pushed out of shape and you are guessing at the four level or higher, there won't be a vicious trump stack. You may get beat with aces and kings and ruffs, but you won't be beat in the trump suit. When this happens, you may not be doubled. The opponents will score their down two or three and wonder who should have doubled.

No one vul. —————————

LHO	Partner	RHO	You
—	—	1 ♡	Pass
1 ♠	Double	Pass	?

♠ 8 2
♡ J 5 4
♢ A Q J 10 9
♣ Q 6 4

When partner shows values plus support for diamonds, this hand starts to look much better. Not only does your suit have value, but your only significant side card takes on a new sheen. You should bid a slightly conservative three diamonds.

LHO	Partner	RHO	You
—	—	1 ♡	Pass
1 ♠	Double	Pass	3 ♢
3 ♠	Pass	Pass	?

♠ 8 2
♡ J 5 4
♢ A Q J 10 9
♣ Q 6 4

With your working maximum, you might feel like bidding to four diamonds. But there are dangers to this worth examining.

First. Partner heard your three diamond bid and he chose not to act. It is likely you are facing a minimum takeout double.

Second. LHO did not raise hearts, so there is the danger that he has one or two hearts. Since RHO did not rebid two hearts, he may have only five. True, he may have six hearts and passed because of a minimum opener. But in my experience, most players tend to rebid two hearts with six card suits no matter what else they have. I would bet that partner has three hearts more than seventy percent of the time. If so, a heart lead will not be good for us in four diamonds.

Third. Since RHO did not raise spades, I don't expect partner to have a stiff. His likely shape is 2-3-4-4.

He has taken his one shot at the auction and has retired.

Even if he has 2-2-4-5 or 3-2-4-4 the hand won't be a bargain at four diamonds. The hand will suffer from duplication in spades, hearts, and to some extent in diamonds. And there won't be any extra values lying around to compensate. To make matters worse, it will be an easy hand for the defense.

One possible setup is this one.

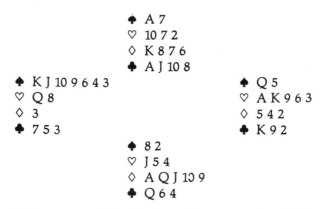

With your wealth of high cards, no one else will have anything extra. Minimums all around the table. It turns out that theirs produces ten tricks on a fortunate lie of the cards, and your minimum produces eight. From your point of view, you can anticipate this, or at least you can anticipate the maximum for your side. What they can make is a little less clear. Their ten tricks are both lucky and coincidental. If you did compete to four diamonds and someone bid four spades, I would consider it a fix. The possibility that they can bid and make four spades should not enter into your considerations.

Vul. vs. not.

LHO	Partner	RHO	You
—	—	1♡	Pass
2♡	Double	3♡*	?

(*not forward going)

♠ 8 2
♡ J 5 4
◊ A Q J 10 9
♣ Q 6 4

The hand gets better and better. Partner has a maximum of two hearts and with RHO's rebid the chances are greatly increased that partner has just one. Even if partner has two, they don't rate to include an honor. RHO's bidding ought to show a good suit if only five long (no promises) so at worst, partner should have two small. It's easy to give partner hands which will pass four diamonds which will make game easily and might even produce a slam.

For starters, partner has nothing (hopefully) in hearts, so his shell will be working. Here are some possibilities.

♠ A 10 6 5
♡ 9
◊ 8 7 5 4
♣ A K 7 3

This makes five diamonds with the trump finesse and may make six with three-three clubs. It is possible that against poor defense, five diamonds will make even with a losing diamond finesse.

♠ K 10 8 4
♡ 3
◊ 8 7 5
♣ A K J 7 3

If the defense doesn't lead a spade early, five diamonds may make. Perhaps it will make anyway.

♠ K Q 5 4
♡ 10 2
◊ K 8 5 4
♣ A J 9 5

Five diamonds would be down two. Unlucky.

♠ A 8 7
♡ 3
◊ K 7 5 3
♣ A K 10 8 3

Slam is cold.

From looking at these example hands, I would lean toward bidding five diamonds for two reasons. There are too many minimum hands which partner can have which make five diamonds cold or good. And when slam is cold, partner may be able to bid it. This is a situation where you have to do a bit of guessing. Five diamonds may make an overtrick or be two off. In this instance, your good trumps may stave off a double.

No one vul.

LHO	Partner	RHO	You
—	1 ◊	1 ♡	3 ◊ *
3 ♡	Pass	Pass	?
			(*limit raise)

♠ 8 2
♡ J 5 4
◊ A Q J 10 9
♣ Q 6 4

A good time to pass. Partner knows your approximate hand and he is willing to play in three hearts. It's true that partner may have a stiff heart and a nice fitting minimum, but if he does, he should be bidding over three hearts. For instance, if you bid four diamonds looking for this hand

♠ A 10 6 5
♡ 3
◊ K 8 6 5 4
♣ K J 7

you shouldn't. Partner would have bid with this hand.

Partner probably has a doubleton heart which will be hard to overcome.

♠ K Q 9 3
♡ 8 2
◊ K 8 7 5
♣ A 10 3

These cards will produce up to six tricks against hearts and they will never stretch to ten tricks in diamonds.

In a situation where you have shown your values, you should usually not take the push unless your values are of exceptional quality. These values are not. You have too much in diamonds, bad shape, no worthwhile side cards, and your jack of hearts is useless. Even worse, if partner has any heart honor, the heart jack will become a defensive trick.

How many hearts does RHO have? Is it possible that he has over-called on a four card suit? On this hand, RHO surely has five hearts. For this reason. Your side has so many diamonds that RHO rates to be short in them. If so, he would not overcall. (See my book on over-calls.) If he had short diamonds, he would lean toward a takeout dou-ble rather than to bid a four-card suit. The importance of this is that if you suspect RHO has a four card suit, then your partner may have three. All the more reason to pass. It would be embarassing to let the opponents push you to the four level with their four-three heart fit.

On this hand, that is unlikely to be happening and I mention it only because the rationale is useful on some occasions.

No one vul. ━━━━━━━━━━━━

LHO	Partner	RHO	You
–	1 ◇	1 ♡	3 ◇ *
3 ♡	Pass	Pass	?
			(*limit raise)

♠ K 2
♡ 9 6 5
◇ Q J 8 7 5
♣ K Q 4

Given this much improved hand, you will not make four diamonds all that often. Even so, with this hand you are far closer to bidding four diamonds than with the previous hand. Everything has improved. Your diamonds have gone up in value. And your black suits are ideal. Still, if partner has two hearts, you won't be much bet-ter than even money. At least you don't have the heart jack, so you don't have a potential defensive trick in their trump suit.

Incidentally, at this stage of the auction, you know partner has at least four diamonds. If you play five card majors, there is always the danger that opener has 4-4-3-2. Here, the opponents have been bid-ding hearts so your partner can't have this specific distribution.

Not vul. vs. vul.

LHO	Partner	RHO	You
1 ♣	1 ◇	3 ♣ *	?
		(*limit raise)	

♠ K 2
♡ 9 6 5
◇ Q J 8 7 5
♣ K Q 4

A trap hand. This is a real piece of junk. With all your high cards and diamonds, I don't expect anyone to pass, but under no circumstances would I bid more than three diamonds. I would expect this to end the auction and I would expect to be down one. If they bid again, they win. I'm through.

There is a lot happening here.

Where are the major suits? RHO doesn't have them. Partner didn't seem interested in them. LHO must have them. LHO could easily be 4-4-2-3. Or possibly he is 4-3-3-3. In either of these cases, they won't make much. Can you tell which case it is? Maybe. Note that opener must have four spades. RHO has three spades at most, you have two, and three in opener's hand would leave partner with five. The only distribution which makes any sense is

Opener	4 spades
Partner	4 spades
RHO	3 spades
You	2 spades

Where are the hearts? Partner probably doesn't have four. And if he had two, the opponents would have bid them. Therefore partner has three hearts. This leaves the hearts distributed

Opener	4 hearts
Partner	3 hearts
RHO	3 hearts
You	3 hearts

And the diamonds? Partner should have five. He doesn't have much in the way of high cards so unless he is goofing off, he ought to have five. This leaves him with one club.

There are one or two possible distributions the opponents can have

4-4-2-3	opposite	3-3-1-6
4-4-1-4	opposite	3-3-2-5

Both of these leave your partner with a singleton club. This is an automatic disaster. If your K Q x of clubs were facing two small, then it would be merely a very poor situation.

Even if you play this in three diamonds, and even if the opening lead is the ace of clubs, these clubs may be worthless. Here is a possible complete hand.

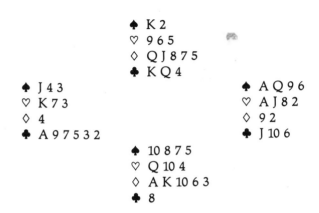

```
            ♠ K 2
            ♡ 9 6 5
            ◊ Q J 8 7 5
            ♣ K Q 4
♠ J 4 3                      ♠ A Q 9 6
♡ K 7 3                      ♡ A J 8 2
◊ 4                          ◊ 9 2
♣ A 9 7 5 3 2                ♣ J 10 6
            ♠ 10 8 7 5
            ♡ Q 10 4
            ◊ A K 10 6 3
            ♣ 8
```

With the lead of the club ace, the defense will shift to a major suit and you will be down immediately. As usual, those values in the opponents' suit were of less than normal value. In this case worthless. If you could trade them in for the queen of spades, three diamonds would be making. Not only were they worthless to you, but their presence in your hand told you that partner was minimum. Therefore you could not reasonably hope for much outside of the diamond suit.

By comparison

Not vul. vs. vul.

LHO	Partner	RHO	You
1♣	1◊	3♣	?

```
            ♠ K 2
            ♡ 9 6 5
            ◊ Q J 8 7 5
            ♣ 9 6 4
```

You work out (as above) that partner is 4-3-5-1. Your hand this time is not very strong in high cards so you can hope for partner to have some working values. If he has something in spades that will be good for you. The important thing is that now, it is a reasonable hope. When you had the K Q of clubs, you just had too many high cards to hope for anything extra from partner.

A practical way of expressing all of this is the following;

Rule. Any time you have wasted cards in the opponent's suit, your partner will be minimum for his bidding.

i.e.

```
            ♠  A Q 10 x x
            ♡  x x
            ◇  K J 10 x
            ♣  x x

  RHO       You       LHO       Partner
                      1♣        Pass
  1♡        1♠        2♡        2♠
  3♡        ?
```

If you choose to bid 3 ♠, you have a better chance of bidding a useful or maximum dummy than if your hand is

```
            ♠  A Q 10 x x
            ♡  Q x
            ◇  K J 10 x
            ♣  Q x
```

Chapter V

THE SPLINTER BID

On many hands when either responder or opener wants to raise, he may be able to do so with a fit-showing jump. This bid shows a fit for partner, a singleton in the suit bid, plus appropriate strength (see ensuing examples).

In the world of conventions, this is known as a splinter bid and I will refer to it as such.

This convention is one of the best around. With the usual caution that a convention is useful only when not abused, I recommend it highly. It has numerous advantages.

1. It pinpoints a control
2. It warns of duplication
3. It provides instant evaluation of a perfect fit
4. It does not compete with other systemic or natural bids
5. It is easy to remember

It is not my intention to get involved in conventions. This is, after all, a book on evaluation — not system. Nonetheless, this convention so strongly lends itself to hand evaluation that I feel obliged to discuss it.

Splinters come up in a variety of standard situations, and there are one or two non-standard ones worth looking at.

The standard situations are these.

Case 1. An unusual jump in an unbid suit. It agrees partner's suit as trump and it shows a singleton in the bid suit. Also, since it is getting the auction up rather quickly, it is a game-forcing bid.

Some example auctions:

LHO	Partner	RHO	You
Pass	1 ♠	Pass	4 ♣

♠ K 10 8 7
♡ K Q 9 6
◇ A 10 6 3
♣ 8

A game-forcing raise with a singleton club. You should not have a *good* five-card or longer side suit. It would be better to show the good suit first and then, auction permitting, to splinter.

LHO	Partner	RHO	You
—	—	Pass	1♡
Pass	1♠	Pass	4◇

♠ A Q 8 7
♡ K Q 10 6 5
◇ 3
♣ A J 5

Values for game, four-card support, and a stiff diamond.

LHO	Partner	RHO	You
—	—	Pass	1♣
Pass	1♠	Pass	3◇

♠ K Q 10 8
♡ A J 4
◇ 3
♣ A Q 10 8 5

Since a reverse bid of two diamonds would be forcing, a jump reverse would show this hand. No need to jump to four diamonds. In fairness, there are various scientific alternatives to some of these bids. But they need be of no immediate concern. If you choose to play splinters, the simple approach will get you ninety percent of the benefits.

LHO	Partner	RHO	You
—	—	Pass	1◇
Pass	1♠	Pass	3♣

♠ Q J 8 7
♡ 3
◇ A Q 10 6
♣ A J 5 4

Three hearts would be an overbid as it is game forcing. Better to bid a nonforcing three spades. Some play three hearts would be a limited splinter forcing only to three spades. Good for this hand, but cumbersome on some others.

LHO	Partner	RHO	You
—	—	Pass	1♠
Pass	2◇	Pass	4♣

♠ A J 8 7 5
♡ A 10 6
◇ K J 9 5
♣ 3

Since partner's two diamond bid promises extra values, you do not need as much strength to give a game-forcing splinter.

LHO	Partner	RHO	You
–	1♠	Pass	2♣
Pass	2♠	Pass	4◇

♠ K 10 7
♡ K 7 6 3
◇ 2
♣ A K 10 8 5

With partner rebidding spades, K 10 7 is quite good enough for a splinter raise. Opposite

♠ A Q 9 8 6 4
♡ A 2
◇ 10 6 3
♣ 9 4

slam will have a decent play. If partner has any useful extras such as a seventh spade or a working queen, slam is cold. And, without the splinter, it will be impossible to bid with assurance.

LHO	Partner	RHO	You
1♡	2♣	Pass	3♡

♠ K J 7 6 5
♡ 2
◇ A 10 5
♣ K J 9 7

No need to restrict splinters to when your side has opened. Slam can exist on good-fitting hands even though the opponents have opened the bidding.

Case 2. Your side has agreed trumps. An unusual jump now is a slam try with shortness in the bid suit.

LHO	Partner	RHO	You
–	1♣	Pass	1♠
Pass	2♠	Pass	4◇

♠ A Q 10 7 6 2
♡ K 8 5
◇ 3
♣ K J 7

This bid shows a stiff, guarantees that the trump suit is adequate, and invites a slam.

73

LHO	Partner	RHO	You
–	1♣	Pass	1♠
Pass	2♠	Pass	4♣

♠ Q J 10 8 7
♡ A K 8
◇ K J 7 6
♣ 2

Most people play that three clubs would be a forcing bid showing a club fit and looking for game. If so, the jump can be used as a splinter, even though it is in partner's first suit.

No one vul.

LHO	Partner	RHO	You
–	–	–	1◇
Pass	1♡	Pass	2♡
Pass	4◇	Pass	?

♠ A K 2
♡ A Q 2
◇ 10 7 6 4 3
♣ 10 8

Not bad! Partner is showing slam interest and he has a singleton diamond. It is not clear what *he* has, but it is clear that what you have is useful. Even though you have only three trumps, you have an excellent hand. I would cue bid four spades which shows both the ace of spades and a willingness to look for slam. Partner won't worry about diamond duplication because you would not have cue bid four spades with an inappropriate hand.

Any time the auction tells you that all of your high cards are working you should be optimistic, regardless of how good or bad they are. You don't know what shell partner is looking for, but you do know you have a good portion of it. If your hand were,

♠ Q J 7
♡ K J 8 7
◇ 8 6 5 4
♣ K Q

a true atrocity, you should feel good about it if you had just heard the given sequence. After

1◇	Pass	1♡	Pass
2♡	Pass	4◇	Pass
?			

you should sign off, but still be apprehensive that you were missing a slam based upon a super fit. Even though you have a terrible, terrible twelve, a totally working twelve is far better than a non-working fifteen or sixteen.

No one vul.

LHO	Partner	RHO	You
—	—	—	1 ◇
Pass	1 ♡	Pass	2 ♡
Pass	4 ◇ *	Pass	?
	(*splinter)		

♠ Q 8 7 5
♡ Q 10 6 2
◇ A K Q
♣ Q 2

With nine points opposite partner's stiff diamond, this hand has ten working points. Sign off in four hearts.

LHO	Partner	RHO	You
—	—	—	1 ◇
Pass	3 ◇ *	Pass	4 ♡
	(*forcing)		

♠ A 8 7 5
♡ 3
◇ A Q 10 8 7
♣ A 10 7

You can cue bid, but it won't be possible to both cue bid and show the stiff heart. Four hearts shows the stiff and slam strength. Your side aces will be implied even though you didn't show them.

LHO	Partner	RHO	You
—	1 ♣	1 ♡	1 ♠
2 ♡	2 ♠	Pass	4 ♡

♠ K Q 10 7 6
♡ 3
◇ K Q 8 7
♣ A 9 5

Same as always. This time, the opponents have bid hearts. But the meaning is the same.

Vul. vs. not.

LHO	Partner	RHO	You
—	—	—	1♣
Pass	1♡	Pass	2♡
Pass	4♣	Pass	?

♠ K 7
♡ K Q 8 7
◇ K 2
♣ 9 7 6 5 4

This is an excellent example of how far you can go in reevaluating a rather boring hand. For starters, this is not even an opening bid. Yet on the auction, anything less than four notrump would be cowardly. If partner has three aces, slam will be playable. And this is just the shell. If partner has a sixth heart or a working queen, slam will be cold. If you do bid Blackwood and find three aces, you should wish them not to include the club ace.

A typical hand for partner:

♠ A J 5
♡ A 10 7 6 5
◇ A Q 4 2
♣ 7

Note that no amount of cue bidding would so enthuse the opener as much as the splinter of four clubs. It is possible that slam could be reached anyway. But given the dog that opener has, he won't be all that excited to cooperate.

Other splinters are not always so obvious. Sometimes the trump suit is understood by implication rather than by agreement.

LHO	Partner	RHO	You
—	1♣	Pass	1♡
1♠	1NT	Pass	3♠

♠ 2
♡ K Q 9 7 5
◇ A 6 4
♣ K Q J 7

Sort of a delayed splinter. In a case like this, partner will stop for a moment and may wonder what's going on. But he should work it out. Especially if splinters are commonly used in the partnership.

I confess an embarassing moment in a situation like this one. My partner and I were also using asking bids. When I bid three spades there was a moment of silence followed by an unsure alert. When asked, partner said it was an asking bid. Confusion! We survived, but that was an accident. From this, I can derive two conclusions. Try to have your system as basic as possible or else have your understandings in order. Also, when your opponent announces an unsure alert, don't ask unless you need to know.

Chapter VI

EVALUATING POOR HANDS

One of the huge advantages the expert has is the ability to evaluate little hands and to exploit them when possible. Most of the time when you have a near Yarborough, or worse, you will pass forlornly or perhaps take an anguished preference when partner demands it. And most of the time, you will be right. But not always.

On occasion, the auction will go in such a way that you are the one who has to make the final decision.

Some of the time, your decision will be whether to save, and in this respect your decision will be easy.

It is much harder when you have to decide that your specific two or three points are just what partner needs to make a game or slam.

Obviously, there is a lot at stake here.

♠ Q 7 5
♡ 10 2
◇ J 7 6 5 4
♣ J 3 2

A terrible hand. What more can be said? Will it help to suggest it could be worse? Goodness knows it could be better. The one thing which is clear here is that partner will have to drag us into the auction. This hand won't go voluntarily.

LHO	Partner	RHO	You
1 ◇	Double	1 ♠	?

♠ Q 7 5
♡ 10 2
◇ J 7 6 5 4
♣ J 3 2

It gets worse. Partner's double meant your black cards were okay, but RHO's spade bid took some of the lustre off the queen of spades. Nothing much good is happening here.

LHO	Partner	RHO	You
1 ◇	Double	1 ♠	Pass
2 ◇	Double	Pass	?

Worse yet. Partner has a very good hand, but it's still hard to like this hand. The one good thing about a bad hand is that it can only go so far downhill. As it is, you actually do have a little something. If you just had a four-card suit, you could start feeling a tiny glow about this hand. I don't know what to bid. Perhaps three clubs, perhaps two spades, even pass. You aren't likely to make anything so you would be content to minimize the size of your loss. Your guess.

LHO	Partner	RHO	You
1 ◇	4 ♡	Double	Pass
Pass	Pass		

♠ Q 7 5
♡ 10 2
◇ J 7 6 5 4
♣ J 3 2

As bad as this hand is, it has a couple of plusses, in a perverse sort of way. First, you have two trumps including the ten spot. This means the double is not based on lots of trump tricks but rather lots of high cards. Secondly, while you don't have anything good for partner, you don't have cards which would hinder the opponents. The ultimate extreme would be this hand.

LHO	Partner	RHO	You
1 ◇	4 ♡	Double	?

♠ Q J 10 9 8
♡ —
◇ K Q J 10
♣ Q J 10 9

The opponents can't make diddly beans. You have potentially seven defensive tricks against them, yet you may have no tricks for partner.

LHO	Partner	RHO	You
1 ♣	Double	2 ♣	Pass
Pass	Double	3 ♣	

♠ Q 7 5
♡ 10 2
◇ J 7 6 5 4
♣ J 3 2

Having passed two clubs the first time around, you have boxed your hand as a bad one. Partner is still interested, and under the circumstances, this hand is a good one. Try three diamonds. If partner raises to four diamonds, you should probably accept. Reevaluation tells you your hand is worth six or seven points and the box principle tells you that you have enough to bid game.

LHO	Partner	RHO	You
1♣	1♡	1♠	Pass
2♣	Double	Pass	3◊
Pass	3♡	Pass	?

Partner's bidding is a little peculiar, but it is obviously showing a good hand. He does not need much from you to make a game. Your heart holding is good enough to raise, but the rest of your hand isn't. If you could turn in your black honors for either red queen, you would have a minimum four heart bid.

Vul. vs. not.

LHO	Partner	RHO	You
—	1◊	2♣	Pass
3♡*	3♠	4♡	?

(*invitational)

Considering that partner has opened and then bid again in the middle of a strong sequence, you have a fine hand for him. The important point is that your spade queen is golden. The more dangerous it is for partner to bid a suit, the more you appreciate honors in his suit. When partner opens one spade, you are happy to have the queen of spades. But when partner bids spades as he does here, your queen is worth even more.

Your diamonds are excellent also. Even with the prevailing vulnerability, you should bid five diamonds. Partner bid three spades fully prepared to hear your preference to four diamonds. True, he may have stretched slightly hoping for a fit. But still, he has to have a good playing hand. Yours is certainly better than it might have been. Much better.

By comparison

Vul. vs. not.

LHO	Partner	RHO	You
—	1◊	2♣	2◊
3♡*	3♠	4♡	?

(*invitational)

♠ Q 7 5
♡ 10 2
◊ J 7 6 5 4
♣ K 10 2

Your hand has been strengthened by the king of clubs. Consequently, you were able to raise diamonds on the first round.

The auction continues as before giving you a similar decision.

This time, you should pass. You have defined your hand and partner knows approximately what you have. Since he is counting on you for some values his three spade bid does not show nearly as much as if you had not raised. If you had suitable values you could bid four spades, five diamonds, or double. This hand falls into none of these categories.

Vul. vs. not.

LHO	Partner	RHO	You
—	1♠	2♣	Pass
3♡ *	4♢	4♡	?
(*invitational)			

♠ Q 7 5
♡ 10 2
♢ J 7 6 5 4
♣ J 3 2

It would be reasonable to bid four spades. No need to bid five diamonds. It's a trick higher. If you were sure diamonds would play a full trick better, then you might bid them. But this is unlikely. More probably, diamonds will be a half trick better. Not enough to increase the level.

Vul. vs. not.

LHO	Partner	RHO	You
—	1♠	2♣	Pass
3♡ *	4♢	4♡	4♠
5♣	Pass	Pass	?
(*invitational)			

♠ Q 7 5
♡ 10 2
♢ J 7 6 5 4
♣ J 3 2

A hard decision. Now that clubs have been raised, it looks like partner will be short, even void in clubs. If he is 5-3-5-0, you may be able to make five diamonds. Or they may be able to make five clubs. Very delicate. On this sequence, you have been able to bid, albeit weakly, so partner knows you aren't totally broke. The question is whether you have any extra playing strength not already shown. I would opt for five diamonds, but with measured conviction. If my jack of clubs were the queen, I would feel this extra defensive potential was enough to sway me. It would not detract from the offensive strength of my hand, but I would not feel that a save was going to be good. If they can't make five clubs, I should bid five diamonds only when I think we can make it. I'm not so confident of this that I would want to risk it.

No one vul.

LHO	Partner	RHO	You
Pass	2♣	Pass	2◇
Pass	2♠	Pass	?

♠ Q 7 5
♡ 10 2
◇ J 7 6 5 4
♣ J 3 2

This is an excellent start toward making something out of this mess. The queen third of spades is taking on as much value as is possible. If the rest of the hand were not so bad, I would raise spades. I actually choose three clubs showing a second negative. Partner will know I have a bad hand for real. Having done this, I hope to be able to jump in spades later to show that as bad hands go, I do have some redeeming feature.

LHO	Partner	RHO	You
—	2♣	Pass	2◇*
Pass	2♠	Pass	3♣**
Pass	3◇	Pass	

(*negative or waiting)
(**second negative)

♠ Q 7 5
♡ 10 2
◇ J 7 6 5 4
♣ J 3 2

The hand has gotten still better. It has gotten so good that I hardly know how to express it. If I had to make a guess, I would guess six diamonds. That's how good the hand has become. This would not be very good bidding, though. Five might be the limit. But also, seven could be cold. What to bid is not so easy. What is easy is to see that this hand has become exceptional.

As with all bad hands, it is hard to fall in love with one. You can look at a queen, or a jack, or a singleton, and think that it ought to be useful. But when you look at the rest of the hand and see nothing but deuces and treys, it can get depressing.

It's wiser to look at the hand from the other side of the table. Here are a couple of hands which partner might have for some of the sequences being discussed. Note how the value of these hands fluctuates according to what partner puts down in dummy.

Hand one

LHO	Partner	RHO	You
—	—	—	1♠
2♣	Pass	3♡*	4◊
		(*invitational)	

♠ K J 9 6 4
♡ A Q
◊ A K 10 9 3
♣ 10

Does partner have

♠ Q 7 5
♡ 10 2
◊ J 7 6 5 4   or
♣ J 3 2

♠ 8 3
♡ 10 7 6 5
◊ J 7 2
♣ K J 8 7

Hand two

LHO	Partner	RHO	You
—	—	—	1◊
2♣	Pass	3♡*	3♠
		(*invitational)	

♠ A K J 2
♡ K 5
◊ A Q 10 8 3 2
♣ 8

Does partner have

♠ Q 7 5
♡ 10 2
◊ J 7 6 5 4   or
♣ J 3 2

♠ 9 7 3
♡ J 8 4 2
◊ 7 6
♣ Q J 5

Hand three

LHO	Partner	RHO	You
—	—	—	2♣
Pass	2◊	Pass	2♠
Pass	3♣	Pass	3◊

♠ A K J 8 6 2
♡ A Q
◊ K Q 10 3
♣ A

Does partner have

♠ Q 7 5		♠ 7 3
♡ 10 2		♡ K 10 5 4 3
◇ J 7 6 5 4	or	◇ 9 6 3
♣ J 3 2		♣ Q 10 4 2

Hand four

LHO	Partner	RHO	You
—	—	—	1 ♠
2 ♣	Pass	3 ♣	3 ◇

♠ A 10 9 6 4
♡ K Q 7
◇ K Q 9 3 2
♣ —

Does partner have

♠ Q 7 5		♠ 7 2
♡ 10 2		♡ J 8 6 4 2
◇ J 7 6 5 4	or	◇ 8 5
♣ J 3 2		♣ Q 10 7 5

In all four cases, the first dummy was of immeasurable value, and the second dummy was worthless.

Hand one would make a game or a low level partscore.

Likewise for hand two.

Hand three makes six diamonds with one dummy and barely offers a play for game with the other.

Hand four is unlikely to produce a game. But when the comparison is between a successful partscore and going down three, the difference is significant.

You should note how much better you feel about

♠ Q 7 5
♡ 10 2
◇ J 7 6 5 4
♣ J 3 2

than about the other four dummies and why you feel this way.

Then, when you find yourself looking at a bad hand and your partner is getting excited over something, see if you can't look at your hand through partner's eyes rather than your own.

When you are debating whether to bid with one of these atrocious hands, it is extremely important to note the context of partner's bidding. Was he under pressure? Was he bidding in a live auction? Was he balancing?

On some sequences, it will be unclear that you are broke. Partner will be justified in hoping you have some values or at least a fit.

On other sequences it will be clear that you have a bad hand so any call by partner will be based on a good hand. He will be hoping for a mild to good fit and will be quite pleased if you have a working king or queen.

LHO	Partner	RHO	You
–	1♠	2♣	Pass
Pass	2♡		

Since this is a balancing auction, partner is not showing more than a sound minimum. He is anticipating that you will have a few values which were inconvenient for you to have bid. He is expecting something from you in the way of high cards and is hoping for a fit.

LHO	Partner	RHO	You
3♡	3♠		

Partner is under some pressure and is being forced to take a position. He has no idea what you have. He is "expecting" at least six or so points and is hoping for more.

LHO	Partner	RHO	You
–	1♠	1NT	Pass
2NT	3♣		

Partner knows the opponents have around twenty-four high card points. He is bidding in a very dangerous sequence so he needs a shapely hand. He doesn't expect to make a game but is hoping for a mild fit. Strategically, it may be that he wants a club lead and is sticking his neck out to get it.

LHO	Partner	RHO	You
–	1♡	1♠	Pass
2♠	3♣		

When the opponents have a fit, your side does also. Partner does not need too much to look for a fit for his side. Since he is at the three level, he won't have a minimum opener but his bidding does not promise the earth.

LHO	Partner	RHO	You
–	1♠	2♢	Pass
3♢	3♠		

Partner is showing a little more than on the previous sequence. Here he is offering only one suit which is more committed than where he is able to offer two. Also, you failed to raise spades the first round so there is a mild suggestion that you don't like them.

LHO	Partner	RHO	You
—	1♠	2♣	Pass
2◊	2♡		

The opponents haven't found a fit so it is a bit more dangerous for partner to act. Since he is offering a second suit he is not showing too much additional.

LHO	Partner	RHO	You
—	1♠	2♣	Pass
2◊	2♠		

This sequence does show extras. The opponents' sequence is less limited than if LHO has raised rather than bid a new suit. Also, their tentative misfit bodes poorly for your side's future should you try to play the hand.

LHO	Partner	RHO	You
—	1♣	1♡	Pass
2◊	2♠		

The reverse principle tells you partner has a good hand. You will have to take a preference to three clubs some of the time on a bad hand. Partner must be prepared for this.

LHO	Partner	RHO	You
1♡	1♠	2♣	Pass
2◊	2♠		

Partner won't have too much high card-wise since the opponents have been able to respond at the two level. He will have very good spades though. Anytime the opponents have shown strength and you have had a chance to raise partner, but declined, then partner will have a good suit when he rebids them.

LHO	Partner	RHO	You
1♠	2♣	2♡	Pass
2♠	2NT		

Partner has a good playing hand with long clubs and four diamonds.

LHO	Partner	RHO	You
2NT	3♡		

Partner does not have a good hand. He probably has a preemptive hand and is just trying to get in the way of their auction.

Some sequences by your opponents clearly define their point holdings, others imply it, and some are a mystery.

LHO	Partner	RHO	You
1NT	Pass	2♡	?

They have 16 opposite zero to seven.

LHO	Partner	RHO	You
–	1♡	1♠	Pass
2♠	3♡	Pass	?

LHO has six to nine. RHO about nine to thirteen.

LHO	Partner	RHO	You
–	1♠	2♣	Pass
2♢	Pass	Pass	?

This one is not clear. RHO has ten to some unclear upper number. He may not like diamonds and have passed a possible misfit. He could have a decent hand. LHO also has unclear values. As little as six and up to twelve. While it is unlikely, the opponents could actually have passed out a combined count of twenty five points. If so, it will be a misfit twenty five points. A good thing your side did not get involved.

It is important to recognize the various types of auctions. Does the bidding suggest you may be broke? Or does it suggest you may have some values? If you can judge what partner's expectations are, you will be able to judge whether you are meeting them, falling short of them, or perhaps exceeding them. Judging the auction and therefore partner's expectations, is as important a part of evaluation as knowing a good from a worthless queen. If partner knows you are broke, and you have a working queen, then you have a good hand. Conversely, there will be times where you have ten, or twelve, or fourteen points, but you will know that partner expected, or hoped for more. Of these two extremes, the important one is knowing when your bad hand is really just what partner ordered.

Perhaps one more example will be useful.

LHO	Partner	RHO	You
3♠	4♡	Pass	?

♠ J 7 6
♡ J 9
♢ K 7 6 5
♣ K 9 4 2

Partner has been forced into taking a position. He may have four hearts made in his own hand. But more likely, he is taking a bit of a risk, hoping you can provide some useful fillers. This hand is about average in terms of meeting partner's expectations. Your hearts will be appreciated by partner. Better you have them than RHO. Also, your kings should be of value. Partner will have some side strength so one or both of your kings will fit in.

LHO	Partner	RHO	You
1♣	Double	1♠	Pass
2♣	2♡		

♠ J 7 6
♡ J 9
◊ K 7 6 5
♣ K 9 4 2

On this sequence, partner is bidding on the merit of his own hand. His double, followed by two hearts shows a very good hand. You could have nothing, but you don't. You have far more than you might. Some players would have bid one notrump with your hand. Even though your cards are devaluated, the club king being almost worthless, you still have a better hand than partner would expect. Your red cards are working, and even though RHO bid spades, your spade jack has some potential.

LHO	Partner	RHO	You
1◊	Double	Pass	1NT
2♣	2♡	Pass	?

♠ J 7 6
♡ J 9
◊ K 7 6 5
♣ K 9 4 2

Your one notrump call showed some strength but LHO's bidding has nullified most of it. Partner is playing you for seven or so points and he is prepared for some wastage in diamonds. He will be disappointed to find wastage in clubs too. Partner reasonably is hoping you have four or five working points. Your hand doesn't have them.

Chapter VII

EVALUATING GOOD BALANCED HANDS

So far, we've looked at weak hands where any action at all has been after strong urging from partner. Also, we've looked at hands of average strength which were not strong enough to initiate action, but which could cooperate with most anything partner could do.

The next set of hands include those where you yourself can take an initial action with future bidding depending on partner's reaction. Some of these hands will be one shot efforts which will rebid minimally, if at all. And others will be strong enough to take further uninvited action. Perhaps there will be extra high cards. Perhaps extra distribution. Perhaps both.

These hands can be broken down into two distributional sets.
1. Balanced.
2. Unbalanced.

And these hands can be divided into three sets of strengths.
1. Minimum of around ten to fifteen points.
2. Good hands of sixteen to twenty.
3. Super hands.

This means there are a total of six sets of hands. I don't claim this is a magic number. Probably, there are closer to a hundred. But these will reasonably cover the field.

THE BALANCED HANDS

Case one. Minimums.

Minimum balanced hands in the ten to fifteen point range do not lend themselves to voluntary action except when in the thirteen to fifteen point range. The ten to twelves will almost always have to wait for an invitation from partner. On occasion, you might try a balancing action, but this is not the same as opening or overcalling.

On those hands which are strong enough to start something, the future of the hand will depend entirely on what partner does. If he makes a non-forcing bid, you will pass. If he invites, you consider whether you have extras. If he forces, you respect it until partner gets tired of forcing. Most of your bids will be straightforward. The only real decisions you will have are when partner invites. Now and then you may have to decide whether to raise partner or to rebid one notrump. But your system will usually answer this question for you.

♠ K 7 5 2
♡ Q J 3
◇ K 2
♣ A 10 8 6

A reasonable thirteen count. As with most balanced hands, if it's good enough to bid, you would prefer to do so via opening the bidding. Or, even better, responding to partner. Hands like this offer no safety and on a bad day, you will go for a large and unavoidable number. For this reason, you will almost never bid when the opponents open. This hand could double a one diamond opening, but it won't take any later action unless forced.

Standard practice dictates you open hands like this with a suit. Some will open with a weak notrump. But they are a minority. Given you take the majority position, and open one club, you will have many opportunities to evaluate your hand. Bidding one club permits you to explore all possibilities, but it also allows the opponents easy access to the bidding. Even though your decisions won't be wide-ranging, you may experience a rapid change in the worth of your hand.

No one vul.

LHO	Partner	RHO	You
—	—	—	1♣
1♡	1♠	Pass	?

♠ K 7 5 2
♡ Q J 3
◇ K 2
♣ A 10 8 6

Your heart holding has gone downhill. But partner has forced. Honor it. Raise to two spades. So far, hand evaluation tells you you have less than you started with. But system does not permit you to exercise any judgment. Yet.

No one vul.

LHO	Partner	RHO	You
—	—	—	1♣
1♡	1♠	Pass	2♠
Pass	3♠	Pass	?

♠ K 7 5 2
♡ Q J 3
◇ K 2
♣ A 10 8 6

Your spade holding is excellent, there being four trumps, not three. Plus you have some slight ruffing values. But your hearts are soft. You should pass.

90

No one vul.

LHO	Partner	RHO	You
–	–	–	1♣
1♡	1♠	Pass	2♠
Pass	2NT	Pass	?

    ♠ K 7 5 2   *A Qxx*

    ♡ Q J 3   *Kxx*

    ◊ K 2   *Qxx*

    ♣ A 10 8 6   *Jxx*

A different problem. Partner has only four spades, but he does have something in hearts. This means your hearts are carrying some weight again. Bear in mind though that your heart values are not contributing to length tricks. Also, with partner showing some length in hearts, there is a danger of RHO getting some heart ruffs. An additional plus is that partner ought to have something in diamonds, so the K 2 will contribute fully. I would be torn between three and four spades, with sympathies to each. Certainly, I feel better about this hand than when partner's game try was three spades. Since partner is counting on me to have something in clubs, I am glad I have the ace. I did open the bidding with one club so partner's notrump call does not promise a club filler.

No one vul.

LHO	Partner	RHO	You
–	–	–	1♣
1◊	1♡	2◊	2♡
3◊	3♡		

    ♠ K 7 5 2

    ♡ Q J 3

    ◊ K 2

    ♣ A 10 8 6

A lot has happened here. Your hearts are very useful now. Q J combinations combine very well with other honors and they stand on their own merit when partner has length but with no honors. Unfortunately your diamond holding has worsened on two counts. First LHO has bid the suit so you already dislike your holding. But it didn't really hit bottom until RHO raised. Before the raise, you were hoping, perhaps vainly, that partner had the queen, or even the ace. RHO's raise implies something in diamonds, so the chances are slight that partner will have any help. The second bad thing to happen is less obvious. With both opponents bidding diamonds, the chances are strong that partner also has a doubleton. It's bad enough that your king is worthless, but now it sounds like your doubleton is also worthless.

This distributional consideration is very important. If partner has no diamond to ruff, he will have an extra black card. It may be a loser. You would far prefer partner to have doubleton queen of spades and three diamonds rather than queen third of spades and two diamonds.

All of these bad things dictate that you pass three hearts. In fact, you may feel that you should have passed the round before. The reason two hearts was chosen was in keeping with the sound principle that you should always try to let partner know when you have a fit. If you fail to raise, partner will not know whether it's safe for him to compete. You may lose once in a while, when you get too high, but you will also lose when your side cannot compete because of no "established" fit.

No one vul.

LHO	Partner	RHO	You
—	—	—	1♣
Pass	2♡	Pass	?

♠ K 7 5 2
♡ Q J 3
◇ K 2
♣ A 10 8 6

Extremely good news. The only soft part of your hand, the Q J of hearts, is now solid. Partner's jump shift will include some number of aces, so your kings are likely going to become prime also. As minimum balanced hands go, this one has become quite fine indeed.

No one vul.

LHO	Partner	RHO	You
—	—	—	1♣
Pass	2♡	Pass	3♡
Pass	3♠	Pass	4♣
Pass	4◇	Pass	?

♠ K 7 5 2
♡ Q J 3
◇ K 2
♣ A 10 8 6

At this stage, every card in your hand is working fully. How you continue the auction is unclear. What is clear is that seven is likely and six must be cold.

♠ Q J 7 5
♡ K 3
◇ K Q 8
♣ Q J 5 2

A generally unappetizing fourteen count. If partner has a bad hand, you are going nowhere. Defensively, it would be disappointing, but not surprising, to see the opponents bid and made a game or even a slam. On the plus side, the hand will be easy to bid. Open a club and rebid one spade. Secondly, whatever partner does will be OK with you. Balanced hands are good from the point of view that you will not end up in a misfit. If partner wants to play in a suit, you have support.

As usual, this hand will not rush to bid if the opponents open the bidding. You could double an opening one heart bid, but you would pass any other call.

No one vul.

LHO	Partner	RHO	You
—	—	—	1♣
Pass	1♡	Pass	1♠
Pass	2♡	Pass	?

♠ Q J 7 5
♡ K 3
◇ K Q 8
♣ Q J 5 2

Like I said. There are not many misfit sequences when you have a balanced hand. This hand has no future. Pass. There are some good things happening though. Since partner is rebidding hearts with no help or implication from you, he should have six or more. Your king doubleton is a fine holding. Also, since partner didn't show any interest in clubs or spades, there is the slight implication that partner has some length in diamonds. Not that he has lots of them, but he ought to have two or three.

No one vul.

LHO	Partner	RHO	You
—	—	—	1♣
1♠	2♡	Pass	2NT
Pass	3♡	Pass	?

♠ Q J 7 5
♡ K 3
◇ K Q 8
♣ Q J 5 2

Your spades are really worthless and as two notrump rebids go, this one has little to offer. Pass. And expect to go down a trick.

No one vul.

LHO	Partner	RHO	You
—	—	—	1♣
Pass	1NT	Pass	?

   ♠ Q J 7 5
   ♡ K 3
   ◇ K Q 8
   ♣ Q J 5 2

Partner had the opportunity to respond in a suit and chose not to. However, he also chose not to raise clubs. Probably, partner has balanced distribution. Also, since a one notrump response to one club shows a little extra, the values you have are likely to combine with something in partner's hand. Pass.

No one vul.

LHO	Partner	RHO	You
—	—	—	1♣
Pass	2NT	Pass	?

   ♠ Q J 7 5
   ♡ K 3
   ◇ K Q 8
   ♣ Q J 5 2

One of the best things that can happen to a balanced hand is to hear partner show significant notrump values. This is a virtual guarantee that your high cards will be working. Some high cards may contribute towards length tricks, some may not. But they will all be contributing something.

No one vul.

LHO	Partner	RHO	You
—	—	—	1♣
1♠	2♣	2◇	?

   ♠ Q J 7 5
   ♡ K 3
   ◇ K Q 8
   ♣ Q J 5 2

A fairly common competitive sequence. When your side has a fit, the opponents will too and they will be climbing into the auction, looking for it. You have to decide whether to continue with this hand or whether to pass.

  Your first impression should be that this hand is nothing special and pass. And I would agree. However, there are some points in favor of bidding.

Here are some pros and cons. Cons first.
1. You have only four clubs.
2. You have some defense against diamonds.
3. Your spades are not worth much.
4. Since RHO did not raise spades, there is the further danger that he can trump one or two spades.

The pros in favor of bidding.
1. Partner usually has four clubs for a raise so you should have a four-four fit. Perhaps even better.
2. This reason is tactical. Where are the hearts? Partner did not make a negative double. If you use the convention then partner's club raise denies four hearts. This means the opponents' fit is in hearts and they have yet to find it. You could try three clubs and hope that the opponents can't find their heart suit.

Weighing the above, I would choose pass because the hand just doesn't make it. If I had a fifth club, or some other small plus, then three clubs could be a winning tactic.

LHO	Partner	RHO	You
—	—	—	1♣
Pass	2♡	Pass	?

♠ Q J 7 5
♡ K 3
◇ K Q 8
♣ Q J 5 2

Partner's jump shift is excellent news, but this hand does not profit as much as it might. It is not clear what partner's intentions are yet. Maybe he has hearts only. Maybe he has hearts and clubs.

In most of my partnerships, we do not jump shift if we have two unbid suits. Therefore, I do not expect partner to have a second suit of spades or diamonds. This means that my spade and diamond cards have less potential than they might. The heart king is certainly good, but there is little more to be happy about. Sufficient to rebid 2NT.

No one vul.

LHO	Partner	RHO	You
—	—	—	1♣
Pass	2♡	Pass	2NT
Pass	3♣	Pass	?

♠ Q J 7 5
♡ K 3
◇ K Q 8
♣ Q J 5 2

A close decision between three hearts and three notrump. I would choose three hearts. This shows support not sufficient to raise the first round. That's all. It is not particularly forward-going. Also, in spite of your strength in both spades and diamonds, neither suit is completely safe from attack. If these are the two hands, three notrump will be in jeopardy.

♠ K 3	♠ Q J 7 5
♡ A Q J 9 7 5	♡ K 3
◇ 7	◇ K Q 8
♣ A 10 7 3	♣ Q J 5 2

This hand will make four hearts virtually 100% of the time. But it will go down in three notrump as often as 20% of the time. The defense leads a diamond to your queen. Your RHO gets in and his diamond return is fatal. To make matters worse, when you do go down in three notrump, you will find that it could have been made.

For example, you win the diamond queen. Do you knock out the ace of spades, or do you take the club finesse? Either could work, either could fail.

The reason I point out the problems of this hand in such detail is that many players overestimate the strength of their stoppers. Sometimes you have to rely on your stoppers to hold up. But sometimes you can explore alternatives. This time you have an easy route to the best contract.

Perhaps if you had the spade and diamond ten spots also, you would not need to bid three hearts. But then, you don't have them.

No one vul.

LHO	Partner	RHO	You
–	–	–	1♣
Pass	2♡	Pass	2NT
Pass	3♣	Pass	3♡
Pass	3♠	Pass	?

♠ Q J 7 5
♡ K 3
◇ K Q 8
♣ Q J 5 2

Despite your foot dragging, partner is still trying. It's nice to know partner has enough to keep slam interests alive, but you still don't have anything to write home about. Bid three notrump. Partner knows you have heart tolerance. But you also have good diamonds which may be worthless except for notrump. It's true that diamonds may be a problem in three notrump. But since you have raised hearts, partner won't be committed to passing. If he passes three notrump, it will be a more knowledgeable decision than if you had rebid three notrump the round earlier.

No one vul.

LHO	Partner	RHO	You
–	–	–	1♣
Pass	2♡	Pass	2NT
Pass	3♣	Pass	3♡
Pass	3♠	Pass	3NT
Pass	5♡	Pass	?

♠ Q J 7 5
♡ K 3
◊ K Q 8
♣ Q J 5 2

More decisions. The first obvious point is that partner is insisting on a slam if we can control the diamond suit. We can. Therefore, we should bid a slam. For the moment, let's ignore *which* slam to bid. That will come later. In the meantime, try this question. How good is this hand in light of the previous bids?

Here is the complete sequence.

LHO	Partner	RHO	You
–	–	–	1♣ (1)
Pass	2♡	Pass	2NT (2)
Pass	3♣	Pass	3♡ (3)
Pass	3♠	Pass	3NT (4)
Pass	5♡	Pass	?

(1) You opened. It's a minimum. At this point partner has no idea what you have.

(2) You rebid two notrump. Your hand hasn't improved particularly. Your two notrump bid might have been made on a goodish hand wanting to hear further from partner. But tentatively, you boxed your hand as some sort of minimum.

(3) When you bid three hearts, it was still possible that you were playing a waiting game. Perhaps you were cue bidding before showing enthusiasm for clubs. Nonetheless, partner is not expecting more than a minimum at this point.

(4) Your three notrump bid is the first genuine signoff bid you have made. But make no bones about it. It is a signoff warning that you have a minimum.

It's still true. You do have a minimum. However, having disparaged this hand at every step, you can stop and appreciate that this ugly duckling does have some hidden merit.

1. Your black suits both have queen jack combinations. These honors reinforce each other and opposite an honor in partner's hand, they have some future.

2. You have the king of hearts. It might have been three small.
3. Your diamonds are K Q 8 rather than K J x.

In the framework of the given auction, this is not too bad a hand.

As to what slam to bid, consider what partner might have. I think he has one of these three hands.

♠ A 2
♡ A Q J 10 7
◇ 6 2
♣ A K 6 3

Six clubs is best.

♠ A K
♡ A Q J 10 7
◇ 6 2
♣ A 10 6 3

Play considerations make this awkward, but six notrump looks best.

♠ A K
♡ A Q J 10 6
◇ 6 2
♣ A K 6 4

Six notrump is a claimer.

Looking at these hands suggests that our minimum will provide at least a finesse for slam and may be enough to claim. What isn't clear is which slam is best. I don't know how to work it out. Of importance, though, are the following.

1. You have diamond control, so according to partner's demand, you must bid a slam.
2. Your hand is far from hopeless.
3. Having offered only belated heart support, your K 3 is guaranteed to be adequate support for hearts.

♠ A 6 2
♡ A 8 5 3
◇ J 5 4
♣ A 8 6

This hand has one thing other minimums often lack. It has three sure tricks. Unfortunately, it has ten losers. Unlike some other minimum hands, it has no potential and to make matters worse, you don't even get to bid your best suit. Most players will open one club and as a result will be starting with a misdescription. Terrible. Yet everyone would open this hand and they would be right.

No one vul.

LHO	Partner	RHO	You
—	—	—	1♣
Pass	Pass	Pass	

♠ A 6 2
♡ A 8 5 3
◇ J 5 4
♣ A 8 6

Bad news. RHO is passing because he has clubs. LHO is passing because he didn't have the shape to act. He probably has clubs too. But it could be worse.

Vul. vs. not.

LHO	Partner	RHO	You
—	—	—	1♣
Pass	Pass	Double	?

♠ A 6 2
♡ A 8 5 3
◇ J 5 4
♣ A 8 6

Now what? If LHO decides to pass, you will go for 1100 opposite a trickless dummy and the auction says that's possible. It's true that you could go for a large number on many routine opening bids, but it's fair to say that if the opponents want to double you, you would prefer to have

♠ K 3	rather than	♠ A 6 2
♡ A 5 2		♡ A 8 5 3
◇ 7 6 5		◇ J 5 4
♣ K Q 10 9 7		♣ A 8 6

No one vul.

LHO	Partner	RHO	You
—	—	—	1♣
Pass	1♠	Pass	1NT
Pass	Pass	Pass	

♠ A 6 2
♡ A 8 5 3
◇ J 5 4
♣ A 8 6

Once again, your hand is no bargain. You can control three suits for sure, and that is better than can be said for many hands you might have. But you have very little in your hand which will benefit from the opening lead. No tenaces. No ten spots. One jack.

No one vul.

LHO	Partner	RHO	You
—	—	—	1♣
Pass	1♠	Pass	1NT
Pass	2NT	Pass	?

♠ A 6 2
♡ A 8 5 3
◇ J 5 4
♣ A 8 6

Pass. My kingdom for two ten spots. Thirteen points is about average for this sequence and can be treated as a maximum or a minimum. If you had any suits which would gain from the lead, you could continue. As I said, add, say, the two black tens, and you have enough to bid three notrump.

No one vul.

LHO	Partner	RHO	You
—	—	—	1♣
Pass	1♠	2◇	?

♠ A 6 2
♡ A 8 5 3
◇ J 5 4
♣ A 8 6

In spite of your bad shape, your hand has been strengthened greatly by partner's bid. He is likely, though no promises, to have five spades. Suddenly a source of tricks. Your three aces are values which are guaranteed. Nothing bad will happen to them. Bid two spades.

Two additional reasons for bidding two spades now are:

1. LHO may raise diamonds.
2. Partner may reopen with three clubs. You will have to pass or correct to three spades, both unappetizing. It is important when you open one of these square hands to raise partner in competitive auctions. This hand with three aces will not be a serious disappointment to partner.

LHO	Partner	RHO	You
—	—	—	1♣
Pass	1NT	Pass	Pass

♠ A 6 2
♡ A 8 5 3
◇ J 5 4
♣ A 8 6

Much better. Now the lead is coming to partner's hand. Far far better to have this hand as dummy in one notrump than as declarer.

LHO	Partner	RHO	You
—	—	—	1♣
Pass	1♡	Pass	2♡
Pass	4♡	Pass	Pass
Pass			

♠ A 6 2
♡ A 8 5 3
◊ J 5 4
♣ A 8 6

Whatever partner has, it will match up nicely with your three aces. Everyone has had the following hand or one like it.

♠ K 3 2
♡ A J 7 6
◊ K 5
♣ K 7 6 4

You open one club and raise partner's one heart to two hearts. He bids four hearts ending the auction. RHO opens the spade queen and the defense grabs three spades when LHO produces the ace.

What happened? What happened was that three of your fourteen points got eaten up by a little misfortune.

Back to the hand with three aces. The shape is poor, but the high cards aren't. Nothing bad is going to happen to them. Maybe the jack of diamonds will go to waste, but that will still mean that twelve out of thirteen points are working. A fine ratio.

LHO	Partner	RHO	You
—	—	—	1♣
Pass	1♡	Pass	2♡
Pass	4◊ *	Pass	?

(*singleton with slam interest)

♠ A 6 2
♡ A 8 5 3
◊ J 5 4
♣ A 8 6

The shell principle works well here. Partner is looking for a slam. You have three aces and a fourth trump. It's obvious that partner is worried about aces. You have them. He thinks slam is possible opposite a working minimum and he can't expect much more than this. I would raise to five hearts or perhaps shoot it out at six.

Vul vs. not

LHO	Partner	RHO	You
—	3♣	Pass	?

♠ A 6 2
♡ A 8 5 3
◊ J 5 4
♣ A 8 6

The strength of aces comes out on hands like this. Partner has a vulnerable preempt, so regardless of what else he has, he has good clubs. This means you can count on seven clubs and two aces. An easy three notrump bid. The only time this bid will lose is when the defense leads diamonds and when they are able to take five tricks. This is not likely to happen. Even if they have five diamond tricks, opener may not have a diamond lead.

Compare the hand with this one. Same auction.

♠ K 7
♡ K Q J 9 5
◊ K Q 10
♣ K 9 7

When partner opens three vulnerable clubs, it is reasonable to hope for a game. But in practice, you may find it unmakeable. Against three notrump, you will probably get a spade lead giving you one spade plus seven clubs. If the defense is inspired, it might lead a red suit and then return a spade through your king. Down three.

This does not have to happen. Sometimes the defense doesn't do the right thing, and you make three notrump. And sometimes it's cold. Partner could put down Q x x of spades. For these reasons, you will bid three notrump and sometimes you will make it. But it's marginal. Your seventeen points made game possible, but because they were slow points, your game was possible at best.

But the hand with three aces provided three fast tricks which were not dependent on other things.

Note that the seventeen point hand won't make five clubs either. The problem? Lack of aces.

Case two. Hands of intermediate strength.

There are actually two categories here. Those which open one notrump, and those which fall between a one notrump and a two notrump opener.

Hands which open one notrump do not have many decisions because the opening bid so concisely defines the hand. Nevertheless, any given one notrump opener can be reevaluated up or down as the result of either partner's or the opponents' bidding.

♠ K J 7
♡ A 10
◊ Q J 10 8
♣ K Q J 7

A seventeen count. Maximum in terms of high cards. Two useful ten spots. The heart ten is especially useful. If you play in notrump, your A 10 of hearts will combine with J x x or Q x x or 9 8 x x to provide two stoppers when LHO leads the suit. Take away the ten and you take away a trick.

You have two suits which can generate tricks. Plus you have good stoppers in both majors. This hand will not require much from partner to come to seven tricks. Lots of potential here. By comparison, if your opening 1NT consisted of

♠ A 9 7
♡ A 8
◊ A 9 6 4
♣ A 5 4 2

you would have four sure tricks, but no clear source of further tricks.

No one vul.

LHO	Partner	RHO	You
–	–	–	1NT
Pass	2NT	Pass	?

♠ K J 7
♡ A 10
◊ Q J 10 8
♣ K Q J 7

Straightforward. Maximum high cards opposite known values. Much of your potential is going to be recognized.

No one vul.

LHO	Partner	RHO	You
–	–	–	1NT
2♡	2♠	Pass	?

♠ K J 7
♡ A 10
◊ Q J 10 8
♣ K Q J 7

Not worth a raise, but you can expect to make it. It's always good news when holdings like K 10 8, Q J x, K J x, etc., are bid by partner. It is especially good news when the overcall does not immediately annihilate some of your values. On this sequence, the only thing better than A x would be two small.

No one vul.

LHO	Partner	RHO	You
—	—	—	1NT
2♦	2♡	Pass	?

♠ K J 7
♡ A 10
♦ Q J 10 8
♣ K Q J 7

Your diamonds are good enough that the opening lead won't hurt them, but they may get ruffed off. Partner's choice of suits leaves something to be desired, but that's life. Possibly you should rebid two notrump, but that's a little bit unusual. Pass and expect to go down. Could be worse. LHO could have bid two spades and partner three hearts!

No one vul.

LHO	Partner	RHO	You
1♣	Pass	1NT	?

♠ K J 7
♡ A 10
♦ Q J 10 8
♣ K Q J 7

Pass. They have their values, even though you have a good hand. Double would be takeout as per the example auction elsewhere. Perhaps that is best because a penalty double probably wouldn't work. Obviously a takeout double is ill-advised because you are poorly placed when partner bids hearts.

No one vul.

LHO	Partner	RHO	You
1NT*	Pass	2♠	?
(15-17 HCP)			

♠ K J 7
♡ A 10
♦ Q J 10 8
♣ K Q J 7

You may have a good fit somewhere, but it's impossible to find sensibly. Best to pass two spades and try to beat it. Bear in mind that RHO can still have six points so you may have one broke partner. Most balanced hands offer as their strength that they will play opposite some fitting cards. If partner has them, good. Here, he may not have them.

No one vul.

LHO	Partner	RHO	You
—	—	—	1NT
Pass	3 ♡	Pass	?

♠ K J 7
♡ A 10
◇ Q J 10 8
♣ K Q J 7

Your maximum will make a game. Your lack of heart support means three notrump is the game. Slightly mixed emotions here.

No one vul.

LHO	Partner	RHO	You
—	—	—	1NT
Pass	3 ♠	Pass	?

♠ K J 7
♡ A 10
◇ Q J 10 8
♣ K Q J 7

Your maximum plus fit will make four spades a reasonable to sure bet. But your lack of side controls means that four spades will be your maximum.

No one vul.

LHO	Partner	RHO	You
—	—	—	1NT
Pass	3 ♠	Pass	4 ♠
Pass	5 ♣	Pass	?

♠ K J 7
♡ A 10
◇ Q J 10 8
♣ K Q J 7

Having boxed your hand as one with spade support, but no interest in slam, you have a good maximum. Bid five hearts.

Not vul. vs. vul.

LHO	Partner	RHO	You
1♣	2♠ *	3♡	?

(*weak jump overcall)

♠ K J 7
♡ A 10
◊ Q J 10 8
♣ K Q J 7

Hard to imagine where everyone is getting their bids. Partner must have the worst weak jump overcall in history or the opponent are nuts. On this vulnerability, I tend to believe the opponents.

How good is this hand? Not too good. Partner is unlikely to have any of the significant prime cards so you may go in with one spade loser, one heart loser, two diamonds, and a club. The defense might lead a club but I don't think they will do so without a stiff or doubleton. If it's a stiff, you could lose the five obvious losers plus a couple of ruffs. I would expect our side to be able to make a maximum of two spades, and the opponents a possible maximum of four hearts. Since they don't have an obviously cold game, I would not do more than bid three spades. And since this doesn't really do much for the auction, it might be best just to pass.

This hand actually came up in a Swiss team. The auction was

LHO	Partner	RHO	You
1♣	2♠	3♡	Pass
3♠	Pass	4◊	Pass
4♡	Pass	4NT	Pass
5♡	Pass	6♡	Pass
Pass	Pass		

No problem. -1430. All these cards came to one trick. Unfortunate, but the opponents' distribution easily compensated for my high cards.

♠ K Q 10 8
♡ A 8 2
◊ K J 8
♣ K J 5

A typical one notrump opener. Near maximum. As with most opening notrumps, there are few sure tricks, but lots of potential. Opposite a yarborough, you may end up with two tricks. Opposite a queen or two, maybe seven tricks. Etc. An unexceptional example.

No one vul.

LHO	Partner	RHO	You
—	—	—	1NT
2♡	2NT	Pass	?

    ♠ K Q 10 8
    ♡ A 8 2
    ◊ K J 8
    ♣ K J 5

Even with a maximum, it would not be wise to continue. All the high cards are nice, but they are not fast. If partner doesn't have two aces, there won't be time to set up and collect nine tricks before they get the heart suit going. In the back of my mind is the possibility that we have a spade fit which we can't find. Annoying.

No one vul.

LHO	Partner	RHO	You
—	—	—	1NT
2♠	2NT	Pass	?

With no fear of the spades, it is clear to bid three notrump. With three stoppers in spades, there will be time to establish and enjoy our winners. There is a mild danger. If LHO finds an inspired heart lead, we may be in trouble. Since this is a theoretical problem only, I would ignore it.

No one vul.

LHO	Partner	RHO	You
—	—	1♠	1NT
2♡	Pass	4♡	?

    ♠ K Q 10 8
    ♡ A 8 2
    ◊ K J 8
    ♣ K J 5

A discouraging auction. In spite of the opening spade bid game for us, or at least a plus score was not out of the question. Now it looks like our plus score has flown. Even with the spade stack, there is little potential for tricks. I would expect them to make four easily and an overtrick is possible. The problem is obvious. Too many kings, queens, and jacks. Not enough aces.

No one vul.

LHO	Partner	RHO	You
1♣	Double	3♣	?

♠ K Q 10 8
♡ A 8 2
◇ K J 8
♣ K J 5

You have an enormous number of high cards for this sequence. Hard to believe. With the club values not working however, it is sufficient to stop in game. Slam may be on, but you will have to find very specific cards in partner's hand. Since LHO may have opened a short club, there is a mild danger that partner has two clubs. My advice would be to choose from four spades or three notrump. Actually, make it four spades. The reason I don't try for slam is, as usual, based somewhat on the wasted club values. They tell me that partner will be minimum. There would be a much better chance of finding partner with extra working values if I didn't have the K J of clubs. Another reason against a slam try is that slam will be questionable and there is no easy way to investigate.

LHO	Partner	RHO	You
2♡	Double	4♡	?

♠ K Q 10 8
♡ A 8 2
◇ K J 8
♣ K J 5

This is much better. Partner has a stiff heart. On the previous sequence, you did not have similar assurance about the club suit. Partner will have a minimum, but there are a lot of ten point shells which make slam cold. Try Blackwood. Note that every single card is working. The only slight flaw is the ace of hearts. It is not combining with anything as are the other honors. But the heart ace will provide a trick.

Not vul. vs. vul.

LHO	Partner	RHO	You
1♠	Pass	1NT	?

♠ K Q 10 8
♡ A 8 2
◇ K J 8
♣ K J 5

There's no future in this hand. Partner has nothing. The good thing about this hand is that they are doing the bidding. Had you been in first seat you would have opened one notrump. Partner might have some small contribution which would let you make it, or he might have an escape suit, but you would never get more than a small plus. Conversely, a large minus is probable. The opponents are sparing you this. Don't give it back.

♠ A 4 2
♡ A 3
◊ K Q J 10 7
♣ Q 9 7

Another one notrump opening. This one has one point fewer than the previous example hand, but it offers more future if partner should have a terrible hand. Against normal misfortune, this hand should produce six tricks.

It does have some flaws. Both major suits are subject to attack. There is nothing to be gained by having the lead come up to your holdings. Your diamond suit is excellent, but it may be too excellent. The ten does not have to be useful. Finally, jacks and queens won't be as valuable opposite your aces as they would be opposite your K J combinations of the previous hand.

Q 7	Q 7
Case A	Case B
A 4 2	K J 5

In case A, the queen has value, but not as substantial as in case B.

No one vul.

LHO	Partner	RHO	You
Pass	1 ♣	Pass	1 ◊
Pass	2 ♣	Pass	?

♠ A 4 2
♡ A 3
◊ K Q J 10 7
♣ Q 9 7

At this moment, slam looks like a distinct possibility. If partner has six clubs A K and nothing else, there will be twelve tricks. If partner also has the ace of diamonds, seven notrump would be cold. This is a typical situation where there are two solid suits to run plus two aces. A grand on only 27 HCP. And biddable too.

But, there are dangers here. The auction

1 ♣	Pass	1 ◊	Pass
2 ♣			

frequently shows a stiff diamond. Partner has six clubs, and he has denied a four card major. 3-3-1-6 is likely. 3-2-1-7 is possible. There are 3-2-2-6 hands to consider also. Some of these would rebid two clubs. Some would rebid one notrump.

If partner has the most likely case of 3-3-1-6, the chances are that he does not have the ace of diamonds. If this is the case, it is unlikely that you will have a slam. The defense will have time to establish a trick before you can get the diamonds going. On an unlucky day, you might not even have a game.

♠ J 3
♡ K Q J
◇ 8 2
♣ A J 10 8 6 4

□

♠ A 4 2
♡ A 3
◇ K Q J 10 7
♣ Q 9 7

A spade lead could defeat both three notrump and five clubs if the club finesse were to fail.

If partner has a better hand, then three notrump may be cold, but six clubs could have no play.

♠ J 9
♡ K Q 9
◇ 3
♣ A K J 8 6 4 2

□

♠ A 4 2
♡ A 3
◇ K Q J 10 7
♣ Q 9 7

You have eleven tricks, and with a spade lead, that will be your maximum.

The result is predictable if you envision partner's stiff diamond. It is another case of duplication. This hand is a hard one to bid. Since seven notrump can be cold, it would be silly to end the auction with a jump to three notrump. I would try two spades and hope to hear something useful.

LHO	Partner	RHO	You
—	1♣	Pass	1◇
Pass	2♣	Pass	2♠
Pass	2NT	Pass	?

110

♠ A 4 2
♡ A 3
◇ K Q J 10 7
♣ Q 9 7

This is mixed news. Partner tends to have minimum values for 2NT. Partner is very unlikely to have a heart stopper plus the diamond ace and club A K. I would rule out seven at this point. My choices now are three clubs, forcing, a simple signoff of three notrump, or perhaps a quantitative raise to four notrump. My own preference would be three notrump and the reason has nothing to do with the evaluation of the hand. I still think slam is possible. The reason I would choose three notrump is that there is no way I can sensibly continue the auction so that partner can make an intelligent decision.

If I bid three clubs, what is partner to do? He may think I have short hearts. He will be worried if he has Q x x. Also, since he is probably looking at a stiff diamond, he will not like it. Whatever he bids over three clubs, he will be doing it for the wrong reasons and I still won't have any useful information.

If I bid four notrump, partner will have a general idea what to do, but I don't expect him to continue. Whatever he has, it is minimumish and he will not like his stiff diamond for a notrump contract. Since I would not expect him to continue very often, and since four notrump will be too high some times, I would reject it.

This leaves three notrump. If you do have a game, this will probably make. One bonus to this is that you will avoid a nerve-wracking auction which rates to gain you very little. Science is good only when you are in control of it. The two spade bid for instance was OK because you were in control of the hand. And you got some benefit from it. Partner is going to play the hand which, considering your major suit holdings, is ideal.

But further science on a questionable hand is overdoing it.

Ever heard a sequence like this?

Partner	You
1 ♣	1 ◇
2 ♣	2 ♠
2NT	3 ♡
3NT	4 ♣
4 ♠	etc.

Where does it stop? Incidentally, if anyone wants to make a jump shift originally, that might solve your problems. Maybe.

Case three. Intermediate plus-18 to 19 points.

Hands in this range fall between opening one and two notrump bids. You open with a one bid and usually rebid two notrump, although other options are available. Since these hands are opened with a suit, you will tend to have more elucidating auctions than after a one notrump bid. A one notrump opening has the effect of keeping the opponents silent, or at least reasonably silent. When you open with a suit, especially a club or a diamond, the opponents tend to get involved. When you have the eighteen or nineteen point hand, the interference isn't too hard to take and you may benefit from it.

No one vul.

LHO	Partner	RHO	You
—	—	—	1♣
Pass	1♡	Pass	?

♠ A K 9 7
♡ Q 2
◇ A 6 5
♣ A Q 7 6

Your rebid choices here are one spade or two notrump. Conceivably, two spades is possible. In practice, I would choose one spade for a variety of reasons.

1. Two spades is excessive. Even with my nineteen points, I can't see forcing to game. If partner passes one spade, I expect it to be high enough.
2. Two notrump is better than two spades because it is not forcing. If partner has a poor hand, two notrump would be high enough. Also, my diamond stopper is too soft. A 6 5 is not a suit you want the lead coming up to.

One spade has a number of merits. It does not lose the spade suit. It does not force us to an unmakeable game. And it permits partner to bid notrump. If partner bids again, and he probably will, we will have no trouble catching up.

There is a certain problem of hand evaluation which is going to be more and more prevalent as your hand gets better and better. Actually, it's not really an evaluation problem. It's an emotional problem. Most hands aren't too spectacular and some of them are downright dull. So when a full-blown nineteen or twenty point hand comes along, it's easy to get excited. Some of the time the excitement is justified. But some of the time it isn't. Obviously, a good hand doesn't need much to go places. When partner produces a decent six count, or more, you end up with a game, or even a slam. Some of the time though, partner doesn't have that six count.

Sometimes he has less. Sometimes he has a lot less. Sometimes he has nothing. When this happens your good hand and your expectations turn into a big bust and a lot of disappointment. This is sad, but it doesn't have to be terrible.

What is terrible is when someone picks up a good hand and drives it forward in spite of repeated denials by partner. A good hand can go only so far on its own merits but eventually, it must run out of gas. If partner is broke, your good hand may run out of gas remarkably early. Usually, partner will have a little something to tide you over and you are forgiven for a little excess enthusiasm. But not always. Sometimes he really has a dog.

I said there was a problem in evaluation of good hands. The problem is that a good many players refuse to accept the fact that their good hand is not as good as they thought it was. These players pick up a good one and totally ignoring their partner's opinions to the contrary, they drive their hand to the moon. When the bubble bursts, and sometimes very loudly, they sit there amidst the pieces and wonder what happened. What happened was they were caught speeding. And what's worse is that they should have known better.

Throughout this book, there has been emphasis on evaluating bad hands and knowing when they are actually good hands. It is a very difficult area of judgment. At least as difficult, and far more painful, is the ability to look at a good hand and to realize when it cannot meet your expectations. The disasters of this variety are often spectacular, being measured in the size of the penalties. -1100, -1700, -1130, etc.

S.J. Simon in his book, *Why You Lose at Bridge*, touched on this briefly and I suspect he would like to have touched on it in far more depth. I for one wish he had done so. I have learned the hard way by paying my dues. I got the experience, 1100 at a time.

$$\spadesuit \text{ A K 9 7}$$
$$\heartsuit \text{ Q 2}$$
$$\diamondsuit \text{ A 6 5}$$
$$\clubsuit \text{ A Q 7 6}$$

LHO	Partner	RHO	You
—	—	—	1♣
Pass	1♡	Pass	?

Getting back to the example hand, it's clear that it is a good one. Yet opposite a minimum response, there may be no game. If partner passes one spade, it is unlikely you have missed anything. But you will get a plus score. By comparison, if you jump shift, you will get to game, but it's academic whether or not it makes.

As I said, a two notrump rebid accurately describes your values, but you may miss a spade contract and you may be playing notrump from the ʍ ong side.

No one vul.

LHO	Partner	RHO	You
—	—	—	1♣
Pass	1♡	Pass	1♠
Pass	Pass	Pass	

To put your mind at ease, here are a few hands partner might have if he passed one spade. Bear in mind that partner won't do this unless he has a reason, *i.e.*, a poor hand.

♠ J 6 4
♡ K 10 7 6 5
◊ J 9 7 3
♣ 10

One spade will make one or two overtricks. Notrump will be a disaster.

♠ 10 6 4 2
♡ K J 7 3
◊ J 8 2
♣ J 3

Just about the best hand partner can have. With anything extra, partner would raise spades. This hand will make a couple of spades, maybe three. Note that a two notrump rebid by opener will end the auction. This will be too high and in the wrong denomination.

Vul. vs. not.

LHO	Partner	RHO	You
—	—	—	1♣
Pass	1♡	Pass	1♠
Pass	2♡	Pass	?

♠ A K 9 7
♡ Q 2
◊ A 6 5
♣ A Q 7 6

This is a good auction for you. Partner doesn't show extra values, but he does show a good suit. Almost always this auction shows six cards. Bid four hearts.

What has happened is that partner's bidding implies a source of tricks not known to you when you rebid one spade. Your Q 2 of hearts is really fine now. As is everything else about your hand. Lots of quick tricks. Note that if you had rebid two spades and partner bid three hearts, you would not be so comfortably placed. Partner had to rebid something since you forced, and his heart suit might have been a compromise rebid. Likewise, if you had rebid two notrump. Now a three heart rebid could be based on a five carder.

114

The important thing here is to appreciate the tremendous improvement in your hand when partner bids and rebids his hearts after your one spade bid.

No one vul.

LHO	Partner	RHO	You
–	–	–	1♣
Pass	Pass	1♡	Double

```
♠ A K 9 7
♡ Q 2
♢ A 6 5
♣ A Q 7 6
```

When partner passed one club, you should be willing to face the fact that you do not have a game. Now, having done that, you should consider whether you have a partscore. Certainly, you can hope for one so you aren't stepping out particularly to double one heart. But you should no longer take the view that it's your hand. It may be. But no guarantees.

No one vul.

LHO	Partner	RHO	You
–	–	–	1♣
Pass	Pass	1♡	Double
2♡	Pass	Pass	?

```
♠ A K 9 7
♡ Q 2
♢ A 6 5
♣ A Q 7 6
```

Well? The box principle works well for you here. Partner denied six points when he passed one club. When you asked him to reconsider, he still chose not to bid. He probably has less than a useful three or four. If you insist, you can double again, but it's beginning to be dangerous. Now, the best you can hope for is a successful partscore. But in reality, you will do well to get away with a small minus.

On hands like this, it is very important to know that partner would bid if he had anything at all. If you can trust him to properly evaluate his three or four point hands, you won't have to take any further risks with this hand.

No one vul.

LHO	Partner	RHO	You
–	–	–	1♣
Pass	Pass	1♡	Double
2♡	Pass	Pass	Double
Pass	2♠	3♡	?

♠ A K 9 7
♡ Q 2
◊ A 6 5
♣ A Q 7 6

Pass. Your opening bid was maximum. Your first double was a normal action. Your second double was a stretch. Bidding again would be a gross overbid. For starters, you have poor shape given your bidding and your hearts are terrible. This hand just isn't the maximum you would need to continue.

Likewise, double would be excessive. You might beat them, but you might not. If partner is broke, and he probably is, you won't beat them more than one. And only then if declarer has the king of clubs.

Both vul.

LHO	Partner	RHO	You
–	Pass	Pass	1♣
Pass	2NT	Pass	?

♠ A K 9 7
♡ Q 2
◊ A 6 5
♣ A Q 7 6

Lots of values here, but since partner is a passed hand, he ought to have a maximum of twelve. The question is whether your prime nineteen can overcome the lack of a couple of points for six notrump. I would say that for want of a long suit, you should sign off at three notrump. If you hate it, try four notrump quantitative. If partner bids a slam, you may make it, but it won't be cold.

No one vul.

LHO	Partner	RHO	You
–	–	–	1♣
Pass	1NT	Pass	?

♠ A K 9 7
♡ Q 2
◊ A 6 5
♣ A Q 7 6

Looks like a three notrump bid. And it is. The reason I am bothering to look at the hand is to see how good three notrump will be. On the plus side is a healthy number of points. But there are some minuses. Partner has denied four hearts and he could easily have two. If so, there is a serious flaw. The defense may run the hearts immediately, or they may set them up and run them later. If you haven't nine tricks quickly, it may not be possible to get them in time. Also, your heart queen may be poorly placed. The expected heart lead could nail it at trick one. There's no way you could reasonably arrange it, but three notrump might have been safer from your side.

The danger inherent in this heart suit becomes more evident when you compare the hand to this one.

No one vul.

LHO	Partner	RHO	You
—	—	—	1 ◊
Pass	1NT	Pass	3NT

♠ A K 9 7
♥ A 6 5
♦ A Q 6 4
♣ Q 2

Here, curiously, hearts are still potentially a problem. The clubs are not. Partner has denied a major suit, hence the concern for hearts. But partner has not denied clubs. He could have anything from 9 7 6 3 to A K 10 7 6 3. Even though this hand and the prior one have exactly the same strength, card for card, this hand gives more assurances.

No one vul.

LHO	Partner	RHO	You
—	—	—	1 ♣
Pass	2 ♣	Pass	?

♠ A K 9 7
♥ Q 2
♦ A 6 5
♣ A Q 6 4

Another typical decision. It looks like there are game values, but even if we have them, it is not clear which game it should be. Three notrump, five clubs, and even four spades are possible. It's entirely possible that all three of these games are on. But perhaps only one will make. It wouldn't surprise me if we had no game at all.

Since partner didn't bid one heart, this suit is obviously a danger. Opposite weak hearts, our game will have to be in clubs or spades. Five clubs is against the odds since it will require eleven tricks. Partner's raise was good news but it did not do so much for your hand that five clubs will be a laydown. And finally, four spades will be on a four-three fit. It will require some specific cards from partner.

The point of the discussion is simple. You have a good hand. Partner has some help. Yet game is not a lock. You should look for one. You might just decide to blast it out with say, three notrump. But you should not be surprised to go down.

In a nutshell, a good hand is good news, but it is not always as good as you may think.

Case four. The big ones — 20 or more.

Since most of the balanced hands in this range are opened with two or three notrump, or some equivalent, there will be fewer opportunities to reevaluate your hand.

However,

$$
\begin{array}{l}
\spadesuit \ \text{A 9} \\
\heartsuit \ \text{K Q 7} \\
\diamondsuit \ \text{K Q J} \\
\clubsuit \ \text{A Q J 5 3}
\end{array}
$$

As the dealer, you would certainly like to hold this collection. It has lots of points, a good suit, and no unstopped suit. Also, it has the nine of spades. This may not seem like a lot, but it does have some potential value. If you play the hand and partner provides you with, say J x x, your nine may provide an extra stopper.

$$
\begin{array}{ccc}
 & \text{J 7 2} & \\
\text{Q 10 8 6 4} & & \text{K 5 3} \\
 & \text{A 9} &
\end{array}
$$

LHO leads his normal fourth best. Dummy plays low and RHO plays the king. You win and in the fullness of time you will get another spade trick. Compare what would happen if RHO traded his five for your nine.

The rest of your hand is also sound. The only soft card is the jack of diamonds and it is hardly a waste.

Your club suit is a distinct asset. All of the honors help to reinforce each other and they will also contribute to length tricks. Lots of plusses all over.

Even so, as fine as this hand is, it must still be measured in terms of its potential. If partner can't oblige with a useful jack or even a ten, you may be in trouble. Even three little clubs would be nice.

Say partner passes your two notrump and partner puts down this.

$$
\begin{array}{l}
\clubsuit \ \text{8 7 2} \\
\heartsuit \ \text{9 6 4 2} \\
\diamondsuit \ \text{8 7 5 4} \\
\clubsuit \ \text{8 2} \\
\quad \square \\
\spadesuit \ \text{A 9} \\
\heartsuit \ \text{K Q 7} \\
\diamondsuit \ \text{K Q J} \\
\clubsuit \ \text{A Q J 5 3}
\end{array}
$$

You win the spade lead and elect to play on clubs. You lead the ace and queen of clubs. RHO wins. Etc., etc. If clubs do not split three three, you may end up with four tricks.

"What happened?," you say. What happened was that you were the victim of poor timing. If left to your own devices, you should be able to get a spade, a heart, two diamonds, and three or four club tricks. Potentially eight tricks. If partner had been able to offer

♠ J 10 x x
♡ x x x x
◇ x x x
♣ 10 x

hardly a selfish request, then two notrump would have some real chances.

No one vul.

LHO	Partner	RHO	You
—	—	—	2NT
Pass	3NT	Pass	Pass
Pass			

Having heard a bid from partner, you know he will offer something for you to work with. Now you can expect the time factor to be more in your favor than it was when partner passed. Note that partner didn't look for a major suit. You have fine minor suit holdings which will match up with partner's minor suit holdings.

LHO	Partner	RHO	You
—	—	—	2NT
Pass	3♠	Pass	?

♠ A 9
♡ K Q 7
◇ K Q J
♣ A Q J 5 3

You got a response from partner, but it is not the response you had hoped for. At least spades are not going to be a concern. The defense won't be running them. The reason three spades isn't such an encouraging bid is that you haven't a fit and this means two things.
1. It may be hard to set up the spades and then get to dummy to use them.
2. If partner has length in spades, he will have shortness elsewhere. If it's in clubs, you may have trouble setting up the club suit.
You bid three notrump, but it won't always be cold.

LHO	Partner	RHO	You
—	—	—	2NT
Pass	3♡	Pass	?

♠ A 9
♡ K Q 7
◊ K Q J
♣ A Q J 5 3

An amazing improvement. Now you can count on the heart suit for up to five tricks. If something good happens in clubs, you may have five of those too. Start cue bidding. The reason the hand has improved so much is that your heart holding tells you that there are sure length tricks available. Also, the adequate trump suit will afford you communication to set up and use the club suit.

Compare these two example hands.

♠ A 9
♡ K Q 7
◊ K Q J
♣ A Q J 5 3

Hand A

♠ 8 6 4
♡ A J 10 8 3
◊ 8 6 3
♣ 10 2

♠ A 9
♡ A K Q
◊ K Q 10
♣ A Q J 5 3

Hand B

♠ 8 6 4
♡ J 10 8 7 3
◊ 8 6 3
♣ 10 2

In hand A, you have communication back and forth via the trump suit. Making six hearts would not be a surprising result although you would not bid it. On hand B, it is conceivable to go down in four hearts, and six hearts will be impossible. The values are the same, but the trump suit is blocked. There's no way to take the club finesse. And, if hearts are four-one, it may not be so easy to draw them. Curiously, six hearts will be bid on hand B rather more often than on hand A because North will get carried away with his twenty six points. In practice, I would be surprised to see anyone get to exactly four hearts. Very hard to achieve this result. More likely, the contract will be three notrump going down, or five or six hearts. At least, five may make against bad defense.

♠ A 6 2
♡ 10 2
◊ A K 5
♣ A K Q 8 2

Another twenty count but this time with fast tricks. You will probably open with two notrump, but it is certainly a maximum in terms of trick taking. You can reasonably expect eight tricks even opposite a yarborough.

That's the good news. The bad news is that the defense may be able to run off the heart suit immediately or they may be able to attack spades. Your hand is good from the trick taking point of view, but it does not rate to gain from the opening lead.

You might think it better to open one club, and on occasion it will be best. For instance, if partner responds, you can arrange the bidding to have partner declare it. Also, you may be able to bid a suit slam which would be unavailable, bidding-wise, if you opened two notrump.

On the other side, one club could be passed out and you would miss a cold three notrump. Or, you might miss a slam, or bid the wrong slam because you could not accurately describe your hand. Hands like this one are typical tough problems which are not easily resolved in Standard American. Much nicer to open one club forcing.

I'm not actually touting a forcing club system. Just thinking how nice it would be on this hand.

♠ Q J
♡ Q 8 3
♢ A K Q J
♣ K Q J 4

One last example of a twenty-one count, this time a bad twenty-one. True, you have four diamond tricks, but your side strength is not going to be productive opposite a yarborough. You may be able to establish a club or two, but by the time you can use them, the defense may have taken as many as nine tricks. You have no stopper in spades and a tentative stopper in hearts.

And defensively, this hand is the worst. If the bidding came up to me thusly,

| 3 ♠ | Pass | 4 ♠ | ? |

I would feel very nervous about bidding. The opponents might be kidding, but if they are serious, they might be able to score up eleven or twelve tricks.

Chapter VIII

EVALUATING GOOD UNBALANCED HANDS

Case one. Hands in the 10 to 15 point range.

Unbalanced hands are somewhat trickier to handle than balanced hands because their value is so speculative. If you pick up a balanced thirteen count, it will grow or diminish in value, according to the auction. But the changes will not be abrupt and they will not often be extreme in range. No matter how the auction goes, your balanced hand will keep some measure of its original value.

Quite the contrary with distributional hands. When you pick up a distributional thirteen count, some of its values will be from singletons or voids. Now, if the auction goes poorly, the value of your hand will go down unbelieveably fast. Likewise, if you find partner with a fit plus some useful high cards, the sky's the limit.

The reason distributional hands reevaluate so drastically is that much of their strength is based on potential, rather than hard values. A singleton. What is it worth? A void? What is a king worth? An ace? Aces and kings are sound values, and they take tricks. Some kings are better than other kings. And some aces are better than other aces.

But have you ever tried to take a trick with a void when the void is in trumps? It can't be done.

Look at this hand.

♠ K 10 7 6
♡ —
♢ K 10 7 6
♣ A 6 5 4 2

If partner opens one spade, conventional wisdom says the void is worth five or six points. This is because you have good trumps and can put the void to work. With this hand, you would force to game and would cooperate in any slam try.

But if the opening bid is one heart, this hand is a very different story. Now the void has minus value because it can't contribute to partner's long suit. Unless the auction takes an upturn, you will be content to accept a part score.

This is in keeping with a basic axiom of hand evaluation.

RULE. Distributional values are subject to much faster and much greater reevaluation than high cards.

Because of the rapid and extreme change in value of shapely hands, it is very important to be able to judge that worth. It is not unlike trying to hold onto a greased pig.

♠ 3
♡ A J 9 7 5
◇ K J 6 4 2
♣ K 3

A typical shapely minimum opening bid. For the moment, there is only hope that partner will support one of our suits. Optimism reigns. Even if the auction goes poorly, the high cards are good and will carry some defensive weight.

No one vul.

LHO	Partner	RHO	You
—	—	—	1 ♡
Pass	3 ♡	Pass	?

♠ 3
♡ A J 9 7 5
◇ K J 6 4 2
♣ K 3

Good news. Slam is possible, although reaching for it might be dangerous. Partner's raise is a fine contribution.

No one vul.

LHO	Partner	RHO	You
—	—	—	1 ♡
Pass	2 ◇	Pass	?

♠ 3
♡ A J 9 7 5
◇ K J 6 4 2
♣ K 3

Short of a jump shift, this response is the best possible. Your diamonds take on the maximum possible value. Also, you have no two loser suit. Note that you have the ace of hearts and the king of diamonds. This hand is better than if you had the K J x x x of hearts and the A J x x x of diamonds.

Compare these two hands.

Hand A	Hand B
♠ 3	♠ 3
♡ A J 9 7 5	♡ K J 6 4 2
◇ K J 6 4 2	◇ A J 9 7 5
♣ K 3	♣ K 3

123

On both hand A and hand B, you open one heart and partner responds two diamonds. In both cases, your hand appreciates in value, but it is clear that hand A has appreciated more than hand B.

RULE. Soft cards go up in value more than hard cards when partner bids that suit.

Accordingly. On hand A, your K J 6 4 2 of diamonds goes from a reasonable holding to an excellent holding. On hand B, your A J 9 7 5 of diamonds also becomes an excellent holding, but because it was worth more in the beginning, the increased value is less.

Note also that the hearts on hand A are better than the hearts on hand B. Even though the two hands have the same high cards, hand A has the edge in value by as much as a couple of points.

No one vul.

LHO	Partner	RHO	You
—	—	—	1♡
Pass	2NT	Pass	?

♠ 3
♡ A J 9 7 5
◇ K J 6 4 2
♣ K 3

This is good news because, while not exactly promising a fit, it does not proclaim a misfit. Since partner rates to have honors in all suits, your minor suit honors are pulling full weight. Hopefully, partner won't have too much in spades. Also, since partner did not bid one spade, he is not likely to have four so he will have his length elsewhere. This will work well for you.

With light distributional hands, you will frequently have an early decision, *i.e.*, whether to open the bidding or to pass and act later. I can offer a simple rule of thumb which will work most of the time.

It is this. If you open and partner responds two notrump, are you happy about it? If you suddenly feel yourself getting cold feet, then you shouldn't have opened.

In practice, no matter what you have to open, you will occasionally wish you hadn't.

Vul. vs. not.

LHO	Partner	RHO	You
—	—	—	1♡
2◇	2♠	Pass	?

♠ 3
♡ A J 9 7 5
◇ K J 6 4 2
♣ K 3

This hand did come up and at this stage in the bidding, I would cheerfully have left the table. Awful. It might be right to take a view here and pass! I wouldn't, but it could be right.

Vul. vs. not.

LHO	Partner	RHO	You
—	—	—	1♡
2◊	2♠	Pass	2NT
Pass	3♣	Pass	?

♠ 3
♡ A J 9 7 5
◊ K J 6 4 2
♣ K 3

This is not getting any better. Only in deference to partner's forcing bids would I continue with this hand. At least partner has a good enough hand to keep bidding. I hope he isn't counting on his shape because his shape and my shape aren't going to be worth anything. Three notrump.

Vul. vs. not.

LHO	Partner	RHO	You
—	—	—	1♡
2◊	2♠	Pass	2NT
Pass	3♣	Pass	3NT
Pass	4♡	Pass	

♠ 3
♡ A J 9 7 5
◊ K J 6 4 2
♣ K 3

Suddenly something good. Partner has heart support and has been describing his shape. He is probably 5-3-1-4 with game values. My hand is going to be something of a disappointment, because I have so much in diamonds.

I don't expect to make four hearts. LHO, who has also heard the auction, will lead a trump. Or he should. And he will lead another one when I lead diamonds. Nonetheless, things are not nearly as grim as during the middle of the auction. At the point where I bid three notrump, it would not surprise me if RHO doubled. Fortunately, it did not come to that.

So far, we've seen how this hand varies in value during a good auction and a horrible auction. In between, there are many common situations where the hand will undergo reevaluation of a less significant, but still important nature.

No one vul.

LHO	Partner	RHO	You
—	—	—	1♡
Pass	1NT	Pass	2◇
Pass	Pass	2♠	?

    ♠ 3
    ♡ A J 9 7 5
    ◇ K J 6 4 2
    ♣ K 3

Partner has expressed a weak hand, but he also has a preference for diamonds. Since he has denied spades or heart support, he will have eight or more cards in the minors. It would not be overbidding to compete with three diamonds. Note that this auction provides quite a few clues to partner's shape and strength. Compare with the following auction.

No one vul.

LHO	Partner	RHO	You
—	—	—	1♡
Pass	1♠	Pass	2◇
Pass	Pass	3♣	?

    ♠ 3
    ♡ A J 9 7 5
    ◇ K J 6 4 2
    ♣ K 3

On this sequence, partner once again shows a poor hand with a diamond preference. However, there is far less reason to believe that the preference is a positive one. Partner could have five or six spades which lessens the number of diamonds partner could have. No one is stopping you from bidding three diamonds, but the risk factor is far greater than on the previous sequence. Where partner responded one notrump and "preferred" to diamonds, it was far more of a positive preference than when he responded one spade and then showed a preference. Also, since partner chose to bid spades, there is extra danger that partner's cards will be in spades and therefore will be wasted. The last thing you want is to find partner with K Q J 7 5 of spades opposite your singleton.

It is very important, when evaluating a hand to consider these two things.

1. How good are your high cards? Are they working? Are they wasted?
2. How will the hand play? Do we have a misfit, or will partner like one of your suits?

No one vul.

LHO	Partner	RHO	You
—	—	—	1♡
Pass	1♠	Pass	2◇
Pass	2♠	Pass	?

    ♠ 3
    ♡ A J 9 7 5
    ◇ K J 6 4 2
    ♣ K 3

A clear pass. Partner is prepared to play two spades opposite a single-ton. You have minimum values and a misfit. Also, you have shown almost everything you have. It's not as if you have some wonderful extra feature still to show.

No one vul.

LHO	Partner	RHO	You
—	—	—	1♡
Pass	1♠	Pass	2◇
Pass	2NT	Pass	?

    ♠ 3
    ♡ A J 9 7 5
    ◇ K J 6 4 2
    ♣ K 3

Here, partner is not denying diamond support. He may have felt two notrump was a better way to show his moderate values. You could rebid three diamonds or you could pass. I would choose pass, but it's close.

One absolutely clear point is that if partner had bid three notrump instead of two notrump, it would be quite poor to continue with four diamonds.

No one vul.

LHO	Partner	RHO	You
—	Pass	1♠	Pass
1NT	Pass	2♡	Pass
2♠	Pass	Pass	?

    ♠ Q 3
    ♡ J
    ◇ Q 10 8 7 5
    ♣ A J 9 5 4

Some of the time the bidding will tell you an enormous amount about partner's hand. This is one such example.

LHO's auction has denied a real interest in both spades and hearts. His major suit distribution could range from 2-1 to 3-3, and I would not expect him to have 3-3 very often. This means LHO has eight cards and possibly more in the minors. If you choose to balance, you will find:

1. Partner has the major suits.
2. LHO has the minor suits.
3. You shouldn't have balanced.

From a high card point of view, partner could have a decent hand. But from a distributional point of view, reopening would be hopeless. Also, you have thirty percent of your strength wasted in the opponents' suits. There is just nothing good to be said about this hand.

There is a very fine knack to knowing when to bid with distributional hands. There is also a fine knack to knowing when to quit bidding with distributional hands. It is especially important with hands in the minimum family because they can't stand on their own merits. Their success or failure will depend on finding something in partner's hand. Knowing when to be optimistic and knowing the danger signals are all part of accurate bidding.

Without regard to specific sequences, it is safe to say that you should be optimistic. Bridge is a bidder's game. You should interpret the above to mean that it is usually right to bid except when you have reason not to. It is a good idea to learn those reasons.

♠ K 10 8 7 5
♡ 3
◊ A J 8 7
♣ Q 10 5

Not worth opening, but good enough to enter the auction if the one level is available.

No one vul.

LHO	Partner	RHO	You
—	—	1♣	1♠
2♣	Pass	Pass	?

♠ K 10 8 7 5
♡ 3
◊ A J 8 7
♣ Q 10 5

What's happening?

Lots.

First, partner is not entirely broke else the opponents would be higher. But he won't have a lot or he would have taken a bid of some sort.

Second. Since LHO did not make a negative double, he does not have four hearts. Opener may have four hearts, but not more. Therefore, your partner has five at least and perhaps six. However, since this is a fit auction by the opponents, your partner would strive to bid if he could. He probably doesn't have six hearts.

Third. Given partner has a few points, he would have raised if he had spade support. Therefore he has one or two spades only.

Fourth. Partner has short clubs except in the event that opener has three and responder four.

Fifth. Partner has four diamonds, or will have them upwards of eighty percent of the time.

In spite of a light overcall, it would be reasonable to persist with two diamonds.

In deciding the worth of your hand, it is important to judge what partner may be able to contribute and where it might be distributionally. When you are the opening side and the opponents remain silent, you can't always judge what is happening. But when the opponents compete, you can sometimes use that fact to advantage.

On those occasions where there is bidding, it is necessary to be able to judge the nature of the auction. Is it safe to bid? Is it dangerous to bid? Which suits are safe, etc., as per the discussion earlier.

No one vul.

LHO	Partner	RHO	You
—	—	1♣	1♠
2♣	Pass	Pass	2◇
Pass	2♠	Pass	?

♠ K 10 8 7 5
♡ 3
◇ A J 8 7
♣ Q 10 5

Your two diamond bid was well reasoned and justified. But the preference to two spades was not what you were hoping for. It means you have probably misjudged partner's diamond length. Perhaps the opponents were on a four-three fit. Or, god help us, a three-three fit. Since partner couldn't raise to two spades voluntarily, it is unlikely that two spades on this sequence will be a good contract. I hope it is not doubled.

No one vul.

LHO	Partner	RHO	You
—	—	1♣	1♠
2♣	Pass	Pass	2◇
3♣	3◇	Pass	?

♠ K 10 8 7 5
♡ 3
◇ A J 8 7
♣ Q 10 5

You certainly will not bid again, but it is worthwhile to estimate your chances of making three diamonds.

Curiously, your chances of making three diamonds depend on whether or not you are using responsive doubles.

First, let's assume you are not using responsive doubles. In this case, your partner may have a reasonable hand.

For instance, he would have

♠ 6 2	or	♠ J 2	or	♠ 2
♡ K 10 7 4 2		♡ A 7 6 5 2		♡ Q J 7 6 2
◇ K 10 6 4 2		◇ K 10 6 3		◇ K Q 10 6 3
♣ 3		♣ 9 4		♣ 9 3

All of these hands will make three diamonds playable or even cold. Note that partner has a decent hand, but no clear way to enter the auction.

If, however, you are using responsive doubles, things change. On all three of the above hands, partner might choose to double two clubs for takeout showing length in the unbid suits. Partner rates to have five hearts (because the opponents didn't look for them). And now he has shown diamond length. If partner had a decent hand with length in the red suits, he would have doubled two clubs. Since he didn't, it is pretty clear that he has a weak hand with compensating shape.

If he has a weak hand, that won't be such good news, but against that, he ought to have a stiff club. LHO raised twice, and he usually doesn't do that without five card support.

On balance, I would not expect three diamonds to make. Most dummies sufficient to make three diamonds would have acted the round before.

Against this, the opponents were going to make three clubs. Possibly, they could even make three notrump. But that's of no practical concern. What is of concern is that LHO may decide to double three diamonds. If LHO has strength in diamonds, he may take a chance. If he doubles, he will probably be right.

No one vul.

LHO	Partner	RHO	You
–	–	1♣	1♠
1NT	Pass	Pass	?

♠ K 10 8 7 5
♡ 3
◇ A J 8 7
♣ Q 10 5

LHO's call tells you your spade suit may not be pulling much weight. Since LHO hasn't looked for hearts, your partner rates to have five or six of them. Since LHO didn't raise clubs, there is a gentle inference that he hasn't active club support. The chances are good that your partner has a few clubs. This means partner won't have much room for diamonds. He might have four of them, but more likely it will be three. Too dangerous to bid two diamonds.

A second reason for not bidding two diamonds is that LHO's one notrump call implies greater high card strength than a raise to two clubs. This diminishes the high cards you could expect from partner.

Part of the problem with shapely hands is that they usually require more than two bids to describe them. Balanced hands, by comparison, can frequently be categorized easily by an opening notrump bid or rebid. Also, when you have shape, so do the opponents. While you are busy showing your shape, the opponents are busy also, so you don't have nice quiet auctions. This is especially so when the strength is divided between you and the opponents.

When you have a hand in the ten to fifteen point range, it is unexceptional for the moment. If partner opens, you can feel the hand belongs to your side. But most of the time, you will be feeling your way, as will the opponents.

With hands of moderate strength, you will be able to compete, but unless partner gets involved, there will be limits to what you can do. The important question is how far you can go without help from partner. Then, if you do get a response, how far can you continue?

The answer to these questions will be based on a number of considerations.

1. What is the value of your honor cards? Are they working? Are they worthless? Or are they of questionable value.
2. Does the auction warn you of a misfit?
3. What strength have the opponents shown? If they have strong hands, your partner will have less than if the opponents have shown weak hands.

No one vul.

LHO	Partner	RHO	You
1♦	Pass	1♥	?

♠ Q 10 8 7 5
♡ 8 7 5
♦ K J 4
♣ K 8

Whether you choose to bid or pass, certain things are obvious.
1. Your diamond values are suspect.
2. Partner's heart values, if any, are suspect.
3. If partner has no club honor, the club king will be suspect.

No one vul.

LHO	Partner	RHO	You
1♦	Pass	1♥	Pass
2♣	Pass	Pass	?

♠ Q 10 8 7 5
♡ 8 7 5
♦ K J 4
♣ K 8

Here, the opponents have a possible misfit, plus, every one of your high cards is dubious. To say nothing of your three small hearts. Pass.

No one vul.

LHO	Partner	RHO	You
—	—	1♥	Pass
2♥	Pass	Pass	?

♠ Q 10 8 7 5
♡ 8 7 5
♦ K J 4
♣ K 8

By comparison, the opponents have a fit and they have limited strength. Also, your high cards are placed behind the strong hand. They rate to be working. Your three small hearts have just become an asset. Bid two spades.

No one vul.

LHO	Partner	RHO	You
1♥	Pass	2♣	Pass
2♥	Pass	Pass	?

♠ Q 10 8 7 5
♡ 8 7 5
♦ K J 4
♣ K 8

The opponents have strong hands. Even though the quality of their fit is unclear, they do have values. Your clubs are well placed, but that's the extent of the good news. Pass.

No one vul.

LHO	Partner	RHO	You
1 ♡	Pass	2 ◊	?

♠ Q 10 8 7 5
♡ 8 7 5
◊ K J 4
♣ K 8

If it was dangerous to reopen on the previous auction when the opponents had stopped in two hearts, it is even more dangerous to act now. Partner has at most a half dozen points and could have less. The opponents have good hands. Consequently, your side does not. At least not in terms of high cards.

It's reasonably easy to judge the worth of your high cards, if you put your mind to it. Not too long ago, a somewhat haughty gentleman picked up this collection.

♠ K J 8
♡ A Q
◊ Q 8 7 5
♣ A K 10 7

It went 1♠-Pass-2◊-? And he couldn't stand it. He doubled. Eleven hundred points later he was explaining to his partner that he had nineteen points and just had to bid. "The result was unlucky."

But was it?

For starters, this hand wasn't worth twenty points because the spades weren't going to carry much weight. But more important, the opponents' auction was dangerous. There was an opening bid plus a two over one response. The only surprising thing about this hand was that a defender could hold nineteen points.

In both *Balancing* and *Overcalls* I went into great lengths to describe what I refer to as "the state of the auction." For a complete discussion, you should refer to one or both books. In the meantime, those points I discussed in an earlier chapter will suffice.

State of the auction

Not to worry. "State of the auction" is hardly complicated. Simply speaking, it works like this. If the opponents are bidding strongly, it will be more dangerous for you to bid than if the opponents are bidding weakly.

If the auction goes, 1♠-Pass-2♣ to you, the possibility exists that they do not have overwhelming strength. They may have it, but they may not.

133

It is possible that they have as little as sixteen high card points. You may reasonably get into the auction with some relatively weak hands.

Conversely, of course, if the opponents are having a strong auction, you will have to be more cautious. After the sequence 1♡-Pass-2♢, you should appreciate that your side won't have more than fifteen or sixteen high card points. If you have ten points yourself, your partner will have zero to four. If you have fourteen, your partner will be broke.

LHO	Partner	RHO	You •
1♡	Pass	2♢	?

♠ K Q 8 7 5
♡ Q 7 6
♢ K J 5
♣ K 3

This is an automatic pass. You have fourteen points to be sure. But like most fourteen point hands, it won't go anywhere if partner hasn't some fillers. On this auction, your partner won't have those fillers. If you are lucky, the opponents will bid on and you will escape. But if you are unlucky, you get doubled and it will be a disaster.

The auction says partner is broke and he probably is.

Safe Suits and Dangerous Suits

There is a second concept which goes hand in hand with safe and dangerous auctions. It is the concept of safe and dangerous suits.

This concept says that on some sequences it will be safe to bid a suit whereas on other sequences, it will be dangerous to bid.

For instance. If the auction goes 1♢-Pass-2♢-? it is safe to say that RHO does not have a major suit worth bidding. Therefore, it is *relatively* safe for you to bid hearts or spades. Opener may have your suit, but at least responder won't have it. Note, though, that RHO has not denied a club suit. If you choose to bid three clubs, you will be a trick higher, and you will be in danger of running into a bunch of clubs in RHO's hand. Here are some possible hands for you to consider that RHO might have

Hand 1	Hand 2	Hand 3
♠ A Q 10 7	♠ 4 2	♠ 4 2
♡ 4 2	♡ A Q 10 7	♡ 8 3 2
♢ Q 10 9 7	♢ Q 10 9 7	♢ Q 10 9 7
♣ 8 3 2	♣ 8 3 2	♣ A Q 10 7

On hand one, RHO would bid one spade in response to one diamond.
On hand two, RHO would respond one heart.
On hand three, RHO would raise diamonds.

This means that when the auction goes 1 ◊ -Pass-2 ◊ , RHO will have a hand similar to hand three rather than one or two.

Similarly, if the bidding goes 1 ◊ -Pass-1NT, it is relatively safe for you to bid hearts or spades because RHO has denied them. But RHO has not denied clubs. In fact, he is a favorite to hold them. Clubs therefore would be considered a dangerous suit.

Without going into intense detail, I will offer a few auctions and suggest thoughts you should have about entering the auction.

1 ♣	Pass	2 ♣

RHO has limited his hand and has shown a fit. This is the safest of all auctions for you to bid on. Strengthwise, it is possible for your side to have a large majority of the strength, plus there are three "safe" suits for you to bid.

1 ◊	Pass	2 ◊

You should feel very much as after 1 ♣ -Pass-2 ♣ . The only difference is that clubs is now a dangerous suit.

1 ♡	Pass	1NT

RHO has shown a limited hand, but he does have some high cards. Clubs and diamonds are dangerous, but still worth bidding. RHO could have good clubs or good diamonds. He might even have both. But he doesn't have to.

Spades, however, is a safe suit and can be bid with a slight degree of impunity.

1 ♡	Pass	2 ◊

This sequence is dangerous because RHO is showing a very good hand. Also, RHO has not denied spades, so there are no "safe" suits. For instance,

Hand 1	*Hand 2*
♠ K J 9 7	♠ K J 9 7
♡ 3	♡ 3
◊ A Q J 7 6	◊ Q 10 7 6 5
♣ Q 10 5	♣ K 4 2

With hand one, responder has enough to bid two diamonds. He would follow it up with two spades if he so judged. On the second hand, RHO hasn't the strength to bid two diamonds so he would respond one spade instead.

1NT	Pass	2NT

No matter what you have, you will be able to tell within a point or two what partner has. If you have eight points, partner will have six or seven.

The point of this is that when you have a hand requiring help from partner, you can often judge from the auction whether partner will have that help. If you are the dealer, and open with

♠ Q 9 7 6 5
♡ K Q 4
◇ K Q 4
♣ Q 2

you do so because you know that partner rates to have something. He may be broke. Or he may have a good hand. You don't know which, but the possibilities are in your favor that partner has something.

But when the opponents bid

1♡	Pass	2♣

you know partner has a near yarborough and won't be able to offer a useful six count.

Some auctions such as a one-over-one are not nearly as defined so you won't have the guarantees of safe suits or safe auctions. For instance,

1◇	Pass	1♠

This response is undefined and can be made on any of these hands.

♠ Q 10 7 6	♠ A Q 10 6 5	♠ A K 7 6 5
♡ 7 4	♡ K Q 9 7 5	♡ —
◇ K 8 7	◇ 2	◇ Q 3 2
♣ J 8 6 5	♣ K 3	♣ A Q 9 6 2

It may be right for you to bid, but there are no implications of safe or dangerous suits nor do you have an accurate estimate of the opposing strength.

No one vul.

LHO	Partner	RHO	You
—	—	1◇	1♠
2◇	Pass	Pass	?

♠ A J 8 7 5
♡ J 9 7
◇ 4
♣ A J 6 3

As light as this hand is, you can still compete. The opponents have a fit and they have limited hands. The only question is what to bid rather than whether to bid.

Since partner doesn't seem to have spade support, it would be a bit nervy to rebid spades. Nor would a committed three clubs be right. Better to reopen with double which keeps open all three suits.

The point of this hand is not really to determine the best bid, but rather to evaluate the auction and to determine that a bid is called for.

It is important to realize that you are not just evaluating your own thirteen cards. You are evaluating the auction as well. On those occasions where the auction is dangerous, then you will evaluate it as such and will not count so much on help from partner. Instead, you will need sound values in your own hand. What is more important is that partner will also evaluate the auction and will know when you are counting on him. If you are, then partner won't hang you when he has a few odds and ends. But if the auction is dangerous, then partner will know you have the goods and will appreciate whatever few gems he may have.

On hands of limited opening bid strength, you will never get involved during dangerous auctions except when holding exceptional shape or a very good suit.

♠ A J 8 7 5
♡ J 9 7
♢ 4
♣ A J 6 3

does not qualify in either way.

If RHO opened one heart, you would overcall one spade. But if the auction continues

RHO	You	LHO	Partner
1♡	1♠	2♢	Pass
2♡	?		

it would be silly to bid again. When RHO opened 1♡, there was no presumption of danger. Overcalling one spade was hardly a safe action, but it was a reasonable one. But when LHO responded two diamonds, the sequence suddenly became dangerous.

Identify the kind of sequence you are facing. It is a very important factor in hand evaluation. If you have

♠ K J 7 6
♡ A Q 9 6
♢ K J 4
♣ K Q

for instance, a nineteen count of moderate description, you can be optimistic regarding game or even slam chances. But if you know partner is broke, you will give up on slam, you will give up on game, and if you are smart, you will give up, period.

When you hold a twelvish point hand with shape it is good news when partner opens the bidding. Since you have shape, you will need more than one bid to describe it. Partner's strength assures you that you will have the opportunity to describe your hand completely.

137

Note these comparisons.

1. When your partner doesn't open, it may not be possible for you to show your entire hand. In fact, it may be too dangerous to show any of it.

2. If instead of a shapely twelve, you had a balanced twelve, you would not feel so inclined to bid if the opponents opened. One nice thing about balanced hands is that it is easy to avoid trouble. Not so with distributional hands.

Consequently, when partner opens the bidding and you have some shape, it is nice to know that you will be able to show all the pertinent features of your hand.

No one vul.

```
♠ A J 8 7 5
♡ J 9 7
♢ 4
♣ A J 6 3
```

Opposite an opening bid, this hand is good enough to think about a game. If partner opens with one heart or one spade, you will drive to game based on your fit and shape. If partner opens a club or a diamond, you will entertain game thoughts. If partner raises spades or shows extra strength you will bid a game. Otherwise, you will invite one.

No one vul.

LHO	Partner	RHO	You
—	1 ◇	Pass	?

```
♠ A J 8 7 5
♡ J 9 7
♢ 4
♣ A J 6 3
```

An easy one spade bid. No problems yet. So far, we have yet to express the strength of the hand or any of its other features.

LHO	Partner	RHO	You
—	1 ◇	Pass	1 ♠
Pass	1NT	Pass	?

```
♠ A J 8 7 5
♡ J 9 7
♢ 4
♣ A J 6 3
```

Still basically an easy decision. Two clubs. Hope partner can bid two spades.

LHO	Partner	RHO	You
—	1 ◊	Pass	1 ♠
Pass	2 ♣	Pass	?

♠ A J 8 7 5
♡ J 9 7
◊ 4
♣ A J 6 3

Easy. Four spades. Ought to be cold or nearly so.

LHO	Partner	RHO	You
—	1 ◊	Pass	1 ♠
Pass	2 ◊	Pass	?

♠ A J 8 7 5
♡ J 9 7
◊ 4
♣ A J 6 3

The toughest decision yet, and even so, not too difficult. Two notrump. Two spades is an underbid. Three clubs is game forcing and the hand isn't worth it. And three spades is wrong because it overstates both the spades and strength. Since partner is likely to have a stiff spade, he ought to have a few hearts so you needn't worry about this suit. Curiously, the suit to worry about is spades. If the defense leads one against a notrump contract, it will probably not be to the advantage of my side.

While these last few problems were not exactly earth-shattering, it is important to notice the nature of the decisions in a non-competitive sequence as opposed to a competitive one. In the problems above, it was clear that you would bid something, and at no time were you particularly concerned with the opponents. There was no danger, no worry that you shouldn't be bidding. And finally, there was no input into your decision from the enemy. You had a clear road in the auction and every decision was carefree and easy.

Compare this to when the auction was

LHO	Partner	RHO	You
—	—	1 ◊	1 ♠
2 ◊	Pass	Pass	?

A few pages ago it was recommended that you double. But this decision was not based so much on the value of your hand as it was based on the bidding. The bidding said to you that it was safe to bid. Your hand had the shape to concur and so you bid again. It was a joint effort.

Perhaps I can give another view of this if I give you a problem without a hand. Just the bidding.

LHO	Partner	RHO	You
–	1◊	Pass	1♡
Pass	1NT	Pass	?

Without looking at your hand, you could easily accept that one notrump might be a good spot.

BUT

LHO	Partner	RHO	You
–	–	1◊	1♡
2◊	Pass	Pass	?

When I hear an auction like this in which the opponents have shown a fit and not too much strength, I very strongly feel that I should be bidding. It is hard for me to believe from this auction that two diamonds is the best place for us to be. I would desperately want to get the opponents higher or perhaps to bid higher myself. It is not the value of my hand which tells me to bid. It is the auction itself which tells me. I would look at my hand to see whether it agrees with what the auction is telling me, and I expect that it would most of the time.

Backtracking again to the prior auction,

LHO	Partner	RHO	You
–	1◊	Pass	1♡
Pass	1NT	Pass	?

The auction tells me nothing except to limit partner's hand, and I could make no sensible decision until I saw my own hand.

Case two. Distributional hands of 16 to 19 points.

Hands of this strength are nice because they can frequently lead to good results opposite a smattering of high cards or even just a partial fit. When partner can respond or make a voluntary bid it is probable that you will end up in a decent contract.

Even so, there are problems with hands in this range, and the solution to those problems will frequently be resolved through intelligent hand evaluation.

1. The first problem is that hands in this range are usually hard to bid. I'm not going to offer any systemic solutions, just the problems.

You open one club and partner responds one spade. Your bid.

♠ K 8 7
♡ A Q 10
◊ 3
♣ A Q 10 8 7 6

You can choose from two clubs,

three clubs,

two spades,

three spades,

two hearts.

You open one spade and partner responds one notrump. Your bid.

♠ A J 10 7 6
♡ A K 5
◇ 2
♣ K Q 7 6

Here you have fewer choices, but they remain imperfect. They are

two clubs,

three clubs,

two notrump.

Annoying.

2. The second problem is easier to handle. It's *how* to evaluate your hand, and whether it is worth pursuing. Or should you give it up.

It is easy to fall in love with hands of 16 to 19 points, and the greater danger is that you will ignore warning signs. When the auction is not going well, there is a tendency to press on and then wonder what went wrong.

Of less frequent occurrence is the incidence of underbidding, which does not happen too often. Usually, the proud owner of an eighteen point hand thinks he has something and he drives the hand forward regardless of outside input. If partner has an average hand or a poor hand, the final contract will be all right or it will be too high. The times the final contract is underbid usually happen because the *partner* of the big hand has underbid.

Partner's problems of hand evaluation are not your problems. Consequently, I don't intend to cover this aspect. It is necessary, though, to be able to trust partner to bid his hand. If you can count on partner to know when his few cards are working, you will not have to take wild shots.

For example, vul. vs. not.

LHO	Partner	RHO	You
—	—	—	1♠
2♣	Pass	2◇	3♡
4◇	Pass	Pass	?

♠ A K J 9 5
♡ A K J 10 7
◇ 3
♣ Q 5

If your partner will bid four hearts with

♠ 8 2
♡ Q 9 6 3
◇ 10 7 5
♣ J 8 7 2

then you can pass four diamonds. Perhaps you will beat it. Perhaps not. But you won't suffer the ignominy of either

1. discovering you are cold for game because partner neglected to bid with

♠ 8 2
♡ Q 9 6 3
◇ 10 7 5
♣ J 8 7 2

or

2. bidding four hearts yourself and finding partner with

♠ 6 3
♡ 6 2
◇ J 10 7 5
♣ J 9 8 6 2

The sour side of the coin occurs when the holder of the eighteen point hand overbids. This is a relatively frequent occurrence, and unfortunately so, because it ought to be avoided.

Occasionally, the opponents can jam the auction forcing you to make a guess. When this happens, you will be right sometimes. Wrong sometimes.

But often, the auction is uncontested, or only minimally so, and a disaster still occurs.

This should not happen.

When you have a good hand, its strength protects it from many assortments of misfortunate happenings. But not all. Fortunately, most of the bad things that happen are predictable and can be anticipated from the information at hand.

♠ 8 7
♡ A Q 9 7 6 5
◇ A Q 7 2
♣ A

A very fine hand which can make game opposite an average five or six count and slam opposite a specific five or six count. All kinds of potential. But because of the broken suits it is vulnerable to bad splits and lack of fillers or fit. Notice that this hand has some specific requirements. The jack of hearts or diamonds will be a significant contribution. The king-queen of clubs would not.

No one vul.

LHO	Partner	RHO	You
–	–	–	1♡
Pass	1NT	Pass	?

♠ 8 7
♡ A Q 9 7 6 5
◇ A Q 7 2
♣ A

You have a nervous rebid problem. Slam is not out of the question.

Responder A

♠ A 6 2
♡ 4
◇ K 10 8 6 3
♣ 8 6 5 4

Game is likely.

Responder B

♠ J 9 5
♡ K 2
◇ J 9 8 3
♣ K J 4 2

But a part score could be quite high enough.

Responder C

♠ Q 6 2
♡ 8 3
◇ 9 6 4
♣ K Q 10 6 3

You will probably choose from among two or three hearts, or two diamonds. I doubt that anyone would stretch to bid three diamonds and I can't conceive of any other choices.

Since this is not a book on systems, I won't explore this any further.

There are some points worth making. However, regarding hand evaluation

1. Partner's one notrump bid, while not forward going in terms of strength or fit, is not a depressing response. Partner may have a prime diamond fit or a secondary heart fit. So far, there has been no bad news. Just lack of good news.

2. Since partner didn't respond one spade or raise hearts, there is a fair chance that he will have a good to outstanding diamond fit.

For the moment, the future of the hand is still in a holding pattern, ready to take off if partner comes through, but content to play a part score if need be.

LHO	Partner	RHO	You
—	—	—	1 ♡
Double	Pass	1NT	?

♠ 8 7
♡ A Q 9 7 6 5
◇ A Q 7 2
♣ A

If you could make four hearts, partner would have been able to find a response of some sort. Probably one notrump or two hearts. Game in diamonds is a distant possibility. But, game is unlikely since LHO has made a takeout double. This action implies some sort of diamond holding. However, in spite of our non-game potential, partner is still likely to have sufficient values to make a part score worthwhile. I would try two hearts and consider following it with three diamonds.

Vul. vs. not.

LHO	Partner	RHO	You
1 ♠	Pass	2 ♠	?

♠ 8 7
♡ A Q 9 7 6 5
◇ A Q 7 2
♣ A

Against a fit auction you can afford to be optimistic. Game may not exist if partner has the wrong cards but it must be safe to venture forward at the three level. This sequence is a little bit like the one in which partner responded one notrump to your one heart. It is similar in that game may exist. The main differences are that the bidding has started at a much higher level for you and the potential for exploration has diminished. Also, if you need a successful finesse in hearts or diamonds, it will likely be offside. Nonetheless, the state of the auction (non-dangerous) says that you should bid something. Either three hearts or double.

LHO	Partner	RHO	You
Pass	Pass	1 ◇	1 ♡
1NT	Pass	2 ♣	?

♠ 8 7
♡ A Q 9 7 6 5
◇ A Q 7 2
♣ A

Mildly dangerous to bid here. LHO claims to have a heart trick and he could easily have two. If so, you may get doubled. This won't be a disaster
144

because you have a good hand with excellent shape and working cards. Your main objective is to buy the hand in two hearts, hopefully making. If LHO continues with three clubs, you should not wave the red flag at him again. Pass and feel that they aren't the favorite to make it. You aren't such a favorite to beat them that you should double. Just feel pleased that you are in position to get a plus.

Note that, on this sequence, it is almost impossible to determine the distribution around the table. You know LHO hasn't four spades, but that is about the extent of it. RHO could have any shape from 4-1-4-4 to 1-2-5-5. LHO has a heart stopper, two or three spades, and some undefined minor suit shape. Since the opening bid was one diamond, LHO would not rush to raise if he had the alternative of one notrump. By comparison, if the bidding were

LHO	Partner	RHO	You
—	—	1♡	1♠
1NT			

you could assume LHO did not like hearts. LHO would not suppress heart support nearly as frequently as support for a minor suit.

Another important point to note here is that partner is nearly broke. If you knew partner had, say, eight points, you could expect him to bid with certain shapes. If he had heart support, he would raise. If he had a good spade suit, he would bid spades. Therefore, if he does neither, he must have a distribution unsuited to bidding. Certain of his hands can be eliminated.

On this auction, you know partner is likely to be broke. Therefore you have available no reasonable inferences about his hand. You are bidding entirely on your own.

LHO	Partner	RHO	You
—	Pass	1♢	1♡
1NT	Pass	2♣	2♡
3♣	3♡	Pass	?

♠ 8 7
♡ A Q 9 7 6 5
♢ A Q 7 2
♣ A

A very peculiar circumstance. Whatever you make of it, partner is limited by his previous pass. Whatever his hand is though, it ought to offer some sort of play for four hearts.

Can you tell what partner has? Since partner doesn't know you have the fine minor suit holding you do have, he won't be bidding on the basis of minor suit cards. Also he is unlikely to have the heart king. Whatever he has, it will be something he thinks is useful. I would guess something like one of these.

♠ A 6 5 4 2	or	♠ K 10 6 3
♡ 10 4 2		♡ 10 6 4 2
◇ 8 3		◇ 9 6
♣ J 5 4		♣ 10 4 2

Either should offer a play for game.

There is an interesting principle here. When you are bidding strongly, perhaps making game invitational noises, you have to consider whether or not partner will be able to evaluate his cards. This is an awkward principle to talk about, so I will show it by example.

LHO	Partner	RHO	You
—	—	1♣	Double
2♣	Pass	3♣	3♠
4♣	Pass	Pass	?

> ♠ A Q J 9 4 3
> ♡ A J 2
> ◇ A Q 9
> ♣ 8

This hand is very near to producing game, but you could go down in three spades if partner has nothing useful. It might be tempting to bid four spades, but that would be a serious error. True, you don't need much, but if partner has what you need, he would have raised. You specifically need help in spades, hearts, and diamonds. That's where partner thinks you need help. And he has heard you bid, unassisted, at the three level. It is clear that partner knows what you need.

By comparison,

LHO	Partner	RHO	You
—	—	1♡	Double
2◇	Pass	3◇	?

> ♣ A Q J 9 4 3
> ♡ A J 2
> ◇ A Q 9
> ♣ 8

Now if you choose to bid three spades, partner will know you have a good hand but he won't know that club values are worthless. Nor will he think too highly of cards in hearts or diamonds. Whatever he does will be for the wrong reason. It is tempting to bid four spades for the reason that partner won't know what his hand is worth.

Similarly,

LHO	Partner	RHO	You
—	—	1♣	Double
3♡	Pass	Pass	?

♠ A K Q J 9 7
♡ A 2
♢ 3
♣ A 10 8 3

Again, partner won't know that his K Q J of diamonds are wasted or that his J 9 4 of clubs is worth two tricks. Don't leave partner with an impossible decision. Bid four spades. This one is clear-cut, whereas the previous hand presented a problem that was sort of theoretical.

Another example.

Both vul.

LHO	Partner	RHO	You
—	—	—	1♠
2♣	Pass	Pass	Double
Pass	2♢	Pass	2♡
Pass	2♠	Pass	3♡
Pass	3♠	Pass	?

♠ A J 6 5 2
♡ K 10 9 4 2
♢ A K
♣ A

Partner knows you need help in the major suits. If he has it, he should have bid four spades over three hearts. You have a good hand, but it is not that good.

RULE. When your bidding has expressly shown where you need help, you should respect partner's decision. The only time you should take a flyer is when partner can't know his cards are working.

Getting back to the hand in question.

LHO	Partner	RHO	You
1♠	Pass	2♣	?

♠ 8 7
♡ A Q 9 7 6 5
♢ A Q 7 2
♣ A

Very unlikely you have a game and hardly likely you will bid it. You need specific cards to make a game and partner, even if he has them, will hesitate to raise. Nonetheless, you should bid two hearts. You may get

147

lucky and hear partner raise. That would be the good news. The bad news, and the likely news, is that the opponents will bid four spades which you won't be able to set.

In the event you do bid two hearts, you should not expect to bid again. Auctions like this featuring a two over one are very dangerous to bid against. You have the values for one bid. But not another. Frankly, if two hearts got doubled, I would not feel good about it.

No one vul.

LHO	Partner	RHO	You
–	–	1♣	1♡
1♠	Pass	3♡	?

♠ 8 7
♡ A Q 9 7 6 5
◊ A Q 7 2
♣ A

Three hearts was explained as showing a strong spade raise with a singleton heart. Your good hand has turned somewhat sour.

Four hearts is decidely dangerous. You have likely duplication in spades. Two opposite two. And if partner's two include the king or queen, it lessens the chance of his having any other working card. Also you are facing a bad trump split. LHO could have three or four hearts to the king.

You could consider bidding four diamonds hoping to direct a lead or perhaps leading to a save. But unless partner has good diamonds, you could be in big trouble. Especially with the known bad break in hearts.

One other bid to reject is double. Your most likely chance to beat four spades is a diamond lead. If you double three hearts, partner will possibly interpret it to mean you want a heart lead in spite of dummy's stiff heart. I would recommend a pass and hope that partner could follow the inferences to a diamond lead. It might not happen this way, but the chances are far better than if you make an emotional double.

No one vul.

LHO	Partner	RHO	You
–	–	1♣	1♡
Pass	Pass	2♣	

♠ 8 7
♡ A Q 9 7 6 5
◊ A Q 7 2
♣ A

Against opponents who are playing negative doubles, as do most tournament players, there is some danger that LHO has a heart stack. If he i
148

waiting to double you it would be foolish to offer him another chance. It is hard to tell what is happening here. Partner's silence tends to deny much of a hand so there is a good chance LHO has some values. If so, his pass can be interpreted as showing a hand waiting to double you.

No one vul.

LHO	Partner	RHO	You
—	—	1♣	1♡
Pass	Pass	2♣	2♢
2NT	Pass	Pass	?

♠ 8 7
♡ A Q 9 7 6 5
♢ A Q 7 2
♣ A

It is not clear that two diamonds was best, but it was not bad at all. What is important is that you appreciate LHO's hand for what it is. He obviously has a decent hand which was worth bidding the round earlier. It is almost guaranteed that he has a ten or eleven point hand with excellent hearts, a single diamond stopper and a smattering of something else.

Both vul.

LHO	Partner	RHO	You
—	Pass	Pass	1♡
Pass	1♠	Pass	2♢
Pass	3♢	Pass	?

♠ 8 7
♡ A Q 9 7 6 5
♢ A Q 7 2
♣ A

It occurred to me in retrospect that the big hand does occasionally underbid. I suspect it is from a lack of appreciation for a nice hand that has become enormous. Evaluating a hand is one thing. Reevaluating it is another. Here, six diamonds would have a play opposite

♠ A 6 4 2
♡ 3
♢ K 10 8 6 3
♣ J 9 5

This is similar to hand A from a few pages previous.

Further, if the defense neglects to lead a spade, six diamonds would be cold opposite

♠ J 10 8 4 2
♡ 3
♢ K J 9 5
♣ K Q 3

149

Maybe science is best and you can find a way to investigate the possibilities. Perhaps you can reach a successful seven diamonds. The main point is that the hand has appreciated enormously.

At the table, though, I have seen this hand, or ones like it, auctioned something like this.

LHO	Partner	RHO	You
—	Pass	Pass	1 ♡
Pass	1 ♠	Pass	2 ◇
Pass	3 ◇	Pass	3 ♡
Pass	4 ◇	Pass	Pass
Pass			

The result was embarrassing, but the post mortem was more so. It consisted mainly of some nonsense about having only sixteen points.

It is hard to determine exactly what this hand is worth, but it must be something in the neighborhood of twenty plus.

The only wasted card is the heart queen, and then only on occasion. If partner has two hearts, you take a finesse. If partner has one heart, the king may ruff out doubleton, helping the establishment of the suit. With the diamond raise, your trumps may be solid, and finally, it is easy to envision where your two little spades will go.

In general, there are problems of hand evaluation which are pertinent to most distributional hands. With shape hands, you are frequently faced with the problem of adequate tricks but not time to get at them. This may happen with balanced hands too, but it is both more infrequent and also harder to anticipate. This for the reason that a balanced hand will have numerous flaws any one of which could prove fatal. Anyway, back to distributional hands.

```
♠  A Q 9 7 6 5
♡  8 2
◇  A K Q 10 7
♣  —
```

Another fine hand with both upside potential and downside disappointment. Holding this hand as dealer I would feel quite comfortable with my chances.

LHO	Partner	RHO	You
—	—	—	1 ♠
Pass	2 ♣	Pass	?

```
♠  A Q 9 7 6 5
♡  8 2
◇  A K Q 10 7
♣  —
```

Good news that partner has values for a two over one. Bad news that his values may not be working.

LHO	Partner	RHO	You
—	—	—	1 ♠
Pass	2 ♣	Pass	3 ◊
Pass	4 ♣	Pass	?

♠ A Q 9 7 6 5
♡ 8 2
◊ A K Q 10 7
♣ —

Suddenly this hand is not only not so good, it is downright questionable. I would bid four diamonds now with more than a little apprehension.

For starters, partner's values are looking more and more like club concentration. When partner responded two clubs, it was not a serious problem, yet. His suit could have been, say, Q 10 8 6 5 4. In which case his side values would be in hearts and spades where I could use them.

Worse, an obvious heart flaw has surfaced. I imagine LHO is already wondering which heart to lead.

LHO	Partner	RHO	You
—	—	—	1 ♠
Pass	2 ♣	Pass	3 ◊
Pass	4 ♣	Pass	4 ◊
Pass	4 ♠	Pass	?

♠ A Q 9 7 6 5
♡ 8 2
◊ A K Q 10 7
♣ —

Inconceivable to bid again. If partner had shown a positive spade fit, it would be very reasonable to try for six spades. But with the actual auction, there is no safety in five spades and there is dubious safety in four. If partner has something like

♠ 10 4
♡ Q 6
◊ J 2
♣ A K Q 8 6 5 4

I will have the pleasure of losing two hearts and some number of trump tricks. Then I will have the option of discarding dummy's A K Q of clubs on my A K Q of diamonds, or I can discard my A K Q of diamonds on dummy's A K Q of clubs. I hope partner will see the humor in whichever I choose.

151

Actually, the auction did not work out badly. Partner was able to find a spade preference which at that stage of the auction was a pleasure to hear. If instead, partner had bid five clubs, I would have to pass and wonder how many heart losers there were, to say nothing of clubs.

LHO	Partner	RHO	You
—	—	1♡	1♠
1NT	2♣	Pass	?

♠ A Q 9 7 6 5
♡ 8 2
◇ A K Q 10 7
♣ —

Another disappointing sequence. It looks right to bid something and I'm sure I will but it's not hard to see that this hand has very limited future. Partner probably has six clubs and from LHO's failure to raise hearts, it is fair to assume partner has four of those too. This doesn't offer much future for either spades or diamonds. I would try two diamonds and would pass three clubs if partner persists.

Hands in any family of strengths present problems in hand evaluation but the problems vary strongly from range to range.

With the little three and four point hands, the problem is usually whether to bid at all.

Hands of higher point ranges usually are easy to bid except when they are put under stress. By this, I mean the case where bidding begins to court danger. Usually this means making a decision. *i.e.*,

Should you go on to game?
Should you make a slam try?
Should you overcall?
Should you double?

For instance, partner opens 1♣:

♠ K J 8 7 5
♡ A 6 2
◇ Q 10 7
♣ 10 8

When RHO passes, there is no problem. You bid an unconcerned one spade. Now, if partner raises to two spades, you have a decision. The point is that some bids are automatic as was the one spade response. And some bids are problems as was the decision of whether to try for game.

Hands in the nine to twelve point range offer quite a few problems. On one side, you may have to decide whether to get into the auction when they open. Or perhaps how far to push when partner does something.

It is not until you get into the decent thirteen plus point hands that it becomes fairly clear to do something. As the hand gets better and better your stance goes from hopeful to quite secure to absolutely demanding.

With the distributional good hands you are usually going to play the hand. Your bidding will occasionally be uncontested and straightforward, such as

1 ♠	Pass	2 ♠	Pass
4 ♠			

but sometimes the auction gets strained, (*i.e.*, misfit or competitive) and you have to make decisions. Usually though, you are just bidding along waiting for a raise or a preference.

In a nutshell, as your hand gets better and better, you go from being a follower to being a leader to being king of the hill.

Which brings us to the enormous distributional hand with game or near game values in hand.

Case three. Exceptionally good distributional hands.

♠ —
♡ A K J 9 7 6 5
◇ A K
♣ A Q 7 5

Anyone holding this hand would feel quite proud of it. Barring a save by the opponents this hand would drive to game and be seriously disappointed if that was the limit. After all, if partner has J x x x of clubs, six clubs will be almost cold. And opposite K x x x of clubs, a grand is likely.

Yet on a bad day, game may not be possible. Facing

♠ Q J 8 7 5
♡ 2
◇ Q 8 6 4
♣ 8 4 2

it is quite possible to see game going down. Even three hearts might be too high.

I doubt I can persuade anyone to stop in a part score. That would be a genuine exercise in pessimism.

But a look at a few sequences may show the dangers of getting higher.

No one vul.

LHO	Partner	RHO	You
Pass	Pass	Pass	2 ♣
Pass	2 ◇	Pass	2 ♡
Pass	2 ♠	Pass	3 ♡
Pass	3NT	Pass	4 ♣
Pass	4 ♡	Pass	?

♠ —
♡ A K J 9 7 6 5
♢ A K
♣ A Q 7 5

So often I have seen this hand come up with some effort such as six hearts, five diamonds, seven hearts even, and God help me, four notrump.

Sometimes declarer gets lucky and makes whatever contract he ends up in. Sometimes he doesn't.

When he doesn't make it, it is usually because the contract was terrible. When it makes, it is because

1. declarer got very lucky, or
2. dummy had an uncommonly good hand.

Both of these reasons should be unacceptable from an aesthetic point of view. If slam is bad, it should not be bid. And if it is good, it should.

As usual in cases like this one, the problem was that the little hand did not express itself accurately and declarer got lucky with his wild jump.

Unfortunately for declarer, there are times when partner has the bad hand commensurate with the auction and it gets filed away under "unlucky results."

Throughout this book I have dwelt on the importance of the little hand bidding up his slim values when appropriate. And the big hand must trust the little hand to do it properly. This is especially the case when one hand has a preponderance of points such as in the example hand. When someone has a shapely twenty-five or so, there won't be much for partner to have. Further, since much of what partner has can be wasted it is necessary that the little hand be able to identify when a specific ace is worthless and when three little in a particular suit is gold.

No one vul.

LHO	Partner	RHO	You
—	—	—	2♣
Pass	2♢	Pass	2♡
Pass	3♢	Pass	3♡
Pass	4♢	Pass	?

♠ —
♡ A K J 9 7 6 5
♢ A K
♣ A Q 6 5

When partner bid two diamonds, there was no cause for alarm. Partner could have values for a grand and still respond two diamonds. In a way, this response is better than a positive response of two spades. This would show length in spades and would detract from the chances of finding heart or club length in partner's hands. Since strength in spades would be useless, you would feel quite unhappy to hear partner respond two spades.

154

Only if he could show side strength would you become optimistic again.

On the second round partner bid three diamonds which creates a very tentative situation. If partner has Q 10 x x x of diamonds, things aren't so good. It may be impossible to use the diamonds in a heart contract, and if diamonds become trumps, the defense may lead spades forcing your A K of diamonds to ruff.

But when partner persists with four diamonds, the jello finally sets. Partner ought to have at least Q J x x x for two rebids. It would not be unreasonable to shoot seven diamonds.

Vul. vs. not.

LHO	Partner	RHO	You
—	—	—	2♣
2♡	Pass	Pass	2♠
Pass	2NT	Pass	3♠
Pass	3NT	Pass	4♣
Pass	5♣	Pass	?

♠ A K Q J 7 3
♡ A 7
◊ A
♣ K Q 8 3

There is a lot happening on this sequence which requires both hand evaluation plus the ability to visualize.

Partner's first pass denied a good hand but when he bid two notrump, he showed his hand wasn't worthless. Under the conventions being used, partner would bid three clubs to show a terrible hand, so he can be counted on for at least six or so. Partner's three notrump bid was another mild disappointment. Game exists, but partner's lack of cooperation implies six spades won't be cold. There is a probable heart loser plus some club cards which will have to go somewhere. The auction so far has little to recommend it except that our hand has not gotten worse.

Finally good news. Partner's raise to five clubs shows at least a four four fit and it could be better.

Now visualization comes into the picture.

With a four four fit there is a strong possibility for slam because now the spade suit can be used to discard dummy's heart losers. Here are a couple of hands which partner may have. Note the differences between a spade contract and a club contract.

♠ A K Q J 7 3	♠ 5
♡ A 7	♡ Q 8 6 4
◊ A	◊ J 9 7 4
♣ K Q 8 3	♣ A 10 5 2

Seven clubs is a good spot. Seven spades on the other hand has no play.

♠ A K Q J 7 3   ♠ 4
♡ A 7   ♡ Q 6 3
♢ A   ♢ 10 9 5 4 2
♣ K Q 8 3   ♣ J 9 6 2

Six clubs is decent while five spades is the maximum.

On the actual sequence, opener should bid 5NT asking about the ace of clubs.

No one vul.

LHO	Partner	RHO	You
—	—	—	2♣
Pass	2♢	Pass	2♡
Pass	3♢	Pass	4♣
Pass	4♡	Pass	Pass
Pass			

♠ K 6 2
♡ A K Q J 10
♢ —
♣ A K Q J 10

This is a rather extreme hand in that it exhibits all kinds of bad things. Firstly, partner's strength is in diamonds where it may be inaccessible. Secondly, dummy won't have four trumps and will seldom have three. This means you won't be able to get any ruffs in dummy. And thirdly, your solid suits won't allow you to get to dummy.

If you are going to make a slam, partner will have to come up with the ace of spades or the queen-jack.

No one vul.

LHO	Partner	RHO	You
—	—	—	2♣
Pass	2♢	Pass	2♠
Pass	3♡	Pass	4♣
Pass	4♠	Pass	?

♠ A K Q 8 7
♡ K
♢ A 5
♣ A K J 9 7

Another good hand which ought to give up. For starters, there may be a spade loser. It is easy to look at this trump holding and think it solid after getting support. But since the support here is likely to have been on two small, the suit may have a loser.

There is a diamond loser and the defense can establish an immediate trick if partner hasn't a diamond card.

True, if partner has the ace of hearts, you will have a discard for the diamond loser. But only if you can get to dummy to use it.

And then, assuming all this comes to pass, you still have holes in the club suit. Here are a couple of likely example hands for partner.

♠ A K Q 8 7	♠ 6 3
♡ K	♡ A J 7 6 4
◊ A 5	◊ J 8 7
♣ A K J 9 7	♣ 8 5 4

Even game is not cold.

♠ A K Q 8 7	♠ J 4
♡ K	♡ Q J 9 8 6
◊ A 5	◊ Q 5 4
♣ A K J 9 7	♣ 10 6 2

Game is cold but slam is extremely against the odds.

♠ A K Q 8 7	♠ 6 3
♡ K	♡ A 8 6 4 2
◊ A 5	◊ K 10 6 3
♣ A K J 9 7	♣ 8 4

Slam is beginning to look possible but it is still nervous in spite of the fact that partner has two key cards. Note that the value of the heart ace and the diamond king is short term. The heart ace provides a trick and makes the heart king a winner. The diamond king is also a winner. But neither helps establish length tricks. You would rather partner had neither honor but instead had some support. Opposite this yarborough, slam is nearly cold.

♠ A K Q 8 7	♠ 6 2
♡ K	♡ 8 6 4
◊ A 5	◊ 8 6 4
♣ A K J 9 7	♣ 6 5 4 3 2

And opposite this one, slam requires only a bit more than two-two clubs.

♠ A K Q 8 7	♠ 6 2
♡ K	♡ 8 6 4 2
◊ A 5	◊ 8 6 4
♣ A K J 9 7	♣ 6 5 4 2

It is really quite incredible how a little thing like two extra trumps is worth more than a working ace and king.

What is happening is threefold with each wrinkle equating to an extra trick. Here is what the extra trumps do.

1. They guarantee, or nearly so, that you have no trump loser.

2. They guarantee no spade loser.
3. They permit you to use the spade suit to discard dummy's diamonds and consequently to ruff your losing diamond.

The reason for this is that you have sufficient trumps to draw them and still have trumps left in both hands. Now you can use your side suit to take discards and later take ruffs in dummy, as in the example hand. By comparison, these two hands do not offer the same situation.

♠ A K J 7 6 5 4	♠ Q 3 2
♡ K Q 7	♡ A 6 4
◊ A 2	◊ J 8 3
♣ 7	♣ A 9 6 2

You have a diamond loser no matter what happens. Even if dummy had another trump and one less diamond, the effect would be the same.

♠ K J 8 2	♠ A Q 10 3
♡ J 7 3	♡ A K Q 8 6 2
◊ Q 4 3	◊ —
♣ A 4 2	♣ K 7 3

This hand will not make seven hearts, but it will make seven spades. You can draw trumps and run hearts ending up with four spades, six hearts, two clubs, and a diamond ruff.

Finally a hand from actual play. As dealer you hold this impressive hand.

♠ A K 10 2
♡ A K Q 9 8 6 5
◊ —
♣ A Q

The auction goes nicely for a while.

LHO	Partner	RHO	You
—	—	—	2♣
Pass	2◊	Pass	2♡
Pass	3♡ !!		

!Amazing! Certainly good news. I will spare you the details, but it turns out that the only makeable slam is six spades. Here are the two hands.

♠ A K 10 2	♠ 9 7 6 3
♡ A K Q 9 8 6 5	♡ J 10 4
◊ —	◊ K J 10 5
♣ A Q	♣ J 9

Spades divided three-two but the club king was offside. One down at six hearts.

I don't propose this hand as a bidding masterpiece but I admit it is not all that clear how to get to six spades. Note that if partner had the queen fourth
158

of spades with no other high cards, seven spades would be the best spot.

What is clear is that the big hand should anticipate the possibility of a four-four fit being superior to the seven-three fit. Unfortunately, it is more complicated than that. If these are the two hands

♠ A K 10 2	♠ Q 8 6 3
♡ A K Q 9 8 6 5	♡ J 10 4
◊ —	◊ 9 7 5
♣ A Q	♣ K 6 2

Then seven hearts is the correct spot. These hands can survive a bad spade split because opener's fourth spade can go on dummy's king of clubs.

Lovely game this bridge.

Both vul.

LHO	Partner	RHO	You
1♣	Pass	Pass	?

♠ A K 10 9
♡ J 10 8
◊ 10 7 6
♣ 10 4 2

□

♠ Q J 8 3
♡ A K Q 7 6 2
◊ —
♣ K 8 5

This hand is one further example of the strength of a four-four fit. On the sequence given, if you arrived in four hearts, you would find ten tricks your maximum.

If, however, you could end up in spades with South the declarer, then twelve tricks would be fairly easy as declarer can ruff two diamonds in hand. And, if LHO starts with a diamond, you might get thirteen tricks if you wish to play aggressively and risk playing for two-two hearts.

When your side has limited strength you won't be able to explore the possibilities too thoroughly because

1. If you can't locate a good fit, you may be too high.
2. The opponents may be bidding too, taking away your room for exploration.

In both of these cases, you may have to be content with an adequate contract rather than trying for the moon.

But, when you side has game-going values with equally divided strength, you can sometimes explore and find the best spot. This is because

1. The opponents are usually quiet.
2. Both you and partner have sufficient strength that you can show the pertinent features.

Even so, there are problems. If you discover a major suit fit, it is often difficult to escape to another suit. Especially when the alternative suit is a minor.

♠ K 8 7 6
♡ 8 6 2
◇ A Q J 3
♣ J 8
□
♠ A Q 10 5 4
♡ A 5
◇ K 10 6 3
♣ A 9

This typical hand makes five spades and will make six diamonds most of the time. But how should it be bid after the auction begins 1♠-Pass-3♠-Pass? Very hard to untangle and I'm not sure how to get about it.

Much of the time it won't matter whether you find the best fit since your considerations are whether to play four of a major or five of a minor. Only when you have twelve tricks in a minor suit will you wish to get involved, and the risk in the search may be that you get to the five level and find this was not the hand for it.

At least when you have evenly balanced strength, one hand may have the inspiration to start looking elsewhere and the other hand may oblige in the search.

A classic example of this is this hand played by B.J. Becker and Dorothy Hayden in the San Francisco Team Trials in 1965.

♠ A Q 9
♡ A J 4
◇ A Q 6 5
♣ Q 10 8
□
♠ K J 8 7 6 5
♡ 10 3
◇ K J 3 2
♣ A

This hand will make exactly twelve tricks at spades or notrump, but will provide thirteen if played in diamonds.

How should the bidding go? Usually it went along these lines.

1♠	2NT
3♠	4NT (showing 18 or 19 balanced)
?	

or

1♠	2◊
2♠	3♠ (game forcing)

After both of these starts, it proved impossible, at least in practice, to escape the lure of spades.

BUT

♠ A Q 9	*Hayden*	*Becker*
♡ A J 4	1♠	3◊
◊ A Q 6 5	4◊	4♡
♣ Q 10 8	4NT	5♣* (0 or 3 aces)
□	5NT	6♣** (0 or 3 kings)
♠ K J 8 7 6 5	7◊	Pass
♡ 10 3		
◊ K J 3 2		
♣ A		

There are a lot of things happening here, but principally the diamond fit and slam values were established before spade agreement. This permitted a direct sequence uncluttered with multiple potential trump suits and ambiguous cue bids.

As I said, a very hard hand to bid. I'm glad I was not sitting East-West at the time.

A second example. Both five spades and six clubs make, and this time it can be bid fairly easily.

LHO	*Partner*	RHO	*You*
–	–	–	1♠
Pass	2♠	Pass	3♣
Pass	4♣	Pass	4◊
Pass	6♣	Pass	Pass
Pass			

♠ K 10 4
♡ J 9 7
◊ 4 2
♣ K J 9 7 5
   □
♠ A Q J 7 6
♡ 2
◊ A 6 4
♣ A Q 10 5

If you don't like the auction, I won't quibble too much, but it seems reasonable to me. What usually happens with hands in this family is that

161

South skips directly to four spades. This makes four or five and South laments in passing that six clubs would have made. And that is the end of the conversation.

And finally, two extreme examples.

No one vul.

LHO	Partner	RHO	You
—	—	Pass	1♠
Pass	2♠ -	Pass	?

♠ K Q 10 8 6 2
♡ —
◇ A Q 3
♣ K J 9 7

I suspect I would just bid four spades and expect to make it. But if partner puts down something like

♠ A 7 3
♡ J 9 6
◇ 4 2
♣ Q 8 6 3 2

I would regret my decision. In fact, the more I look at this dummy the more I think that your rebid should be three clubs.

The key here is that you have total control of the auction. If the miracle fit exists, you should be able to find out and if it doesn't exist, you won't be getting too high.

Both vul.

LHO	Partner	RHO	You
—	—	—	1♡
Pass	2♡	Pass	3♣
Pass	4◇ !!		

♠ 3
♡ A K Q 8 7
◇ J 9 7
♣ A K J 4

This time, your exploration bid hits gold via a splinter. Since partner has at most the jack of hearts, he probably has an ace plus the queen fourth or fifth of clubs. In practice, his hand turned out to be

♠ A 6 2
♡ J 9 6
◇ 3
♣ Q 10 8 6 5 2

Slam is cold in either hearts or clubs. Again, notice that the slam exploration could be kept at a safe level. Only if partner showed strong enthusiasm would you get beyond your safety level of four hearts. Further, your auction was calculated to let partner know what specific cards you needed and he had a convenient way to show them.

In the third case where one hand has a mountain and the other hand a yarborough, it is hard to locate the best fit for yet another reason. The little hand often has few or no points at all and his bids must be used to deny values rather than show length. Often responder has some suit such as J 8 7 4 2 or even better and the auction does not permit him to show it. For instance, how should these hands be bid?

♠ 8 7 5
♡ J 2
◊ 9 7 4
♣ Q J 8 3 2

□

♠ A K 8 2
♡ A K Q 5 4
◊ 3
♣ A K 9

Six clubs is cold, but I expect this would be the auction at a great many tables:

North	South
Pass	2 ♣
2 ◊	2 ♡
3 ♣ *	3 ♠
4 ♡	Pass

(*second negative showing a genuinely poor hand)

It's easy to say that South should bid again over four hearts, but if North has the same hand but with the minor suits reversed, even four hearts will be in jeopardy.

Maybe a forcing club structure would get to slam.

Retrieving this hand from a few pages ago,

	North	South
♠ 9 7 6 2		
♡ J 10 4	Pass	2♣
◊ K J 10 5	2◊	2♡
♣ J 9	3♡	?

□

♠ A K 10 2
♡ A K Q 9 7 6 5
◊ —
♣ A Q

If South tries to introduce spades, North may think South is cue bidding and not show his four small cards. This will lead to some number of hearts which may or may not be best. True, North and South may end up in spades, but I have seen good pairs floundering in sequences like this one. They would not reach six spades with any overwhelming confidence.

Curiously, if North had a weaker hand, it would be easy to reach six or seven spades.

♠ 9 7 6 3
♡ 10 4
◊ J 9 7 5
♣ J 9 2

□

♠ A K 10 2
♡ A K Q 9 7 6 5
◊ —
♣ A Q

The bidding would go:

North	South	
Pass	2♣	
2◊	2♡	
3♣*	3♠	(*second negative)
4♠	5NT**	(**How good are your trumps?)
6♣***	6♠	(***bad)

South could expect to make six or seven spades depending on whether North had the spade queen or not.

Chapter IX

EXERCISES IN EVALUATION

```
♠ 9 7 4
♡ —
◇ Q J 9 7
♣ A 10 9 8 5 4
```

Before the auction begins, you have no idea what hands like this are worth. The shape suggests more potential than a balanced twelve count, but if no fit exists, this hand can work our poorly. It is a distinct plus to have the high cards in your long suits. This hand is worth far more than, say,

```
♠ A Q 9
♡ —
◇ J 9 7 4
♣ 10 8 7 4 3 2
```

LHO	Partner	RHO	You
Pass	1♠	Pass	2♣
Pass	3♡	Pass	?

```
♠ 9 7 4
♡ —
◇ Q J 9 7
♣ A 10 9 8 5 4
```

I haven't the slightest idea what to do here. The void in hearts looks nice, but if partner has to ruff a bunch of hearts, my hand may not be so good. The defense will be able to lead trumps leaving partner with quite a few losers. The answer to whether you should bid game depends on what partner has in the minors. If he has ◇K x x, my hand may be good. I would bid four spades, but would worry somewhat until I could see how the play was going.

Note this pair of hands.

```
♠ 8 7 5            ♠ 8 7 5
♡ —               ♡ 10 4
◇ 8 6 5 4 2        ◇ 8 6 5 4
♣ 10 7 5 3 2       ♣ 7 5 3 2
      □                  □
♠ A K 9 6 4        ♠ A K 9 6 4
♡ A K 8 5 2        ♡ A K 8 5 2
◇ J 3             ◇ J 3
♣ 9               ♣ 9
```

Spades are trumps in both cases. In the first pair of hands, dummy probably thought his heart void had some value, but it did not. Declarer would have preferred to find the dummy in the second example. Both hands could end up producing nine tricks, but if trumps are led initially, the first hand will take no more than eight. This setup simply demonstrates that voids can be worth a lot less than normally expected.

LHO	Partner	RHO	You
1♡	2◇	2♡	?

♠ 9 7 4
♡ —
◇ Q J 9 7
♣ A 10 9 8 5 4

On this sequence, the hand acquires much much more value than when partner was bidding spades. There are a number of reasons for this.

First, you have a fourth trump which means you automatically get one more ruff than if you had only three trumps. This assuming partner intends to ruff hearts.

Secondly, you have a side suit which can be set up. With your four trumps, you can hope to be able to draw trumps and run the club suit. When spades were trumps, this option was not as clear cut.

Thirdly, the opponents' heart bidding gently suggests partner doesn't have wasted heart honors. There is no guarantee of this, but RHO's raise contributes to the possibility.

There is a lot to be said for jumping to five diamonds, but if partner does have a lot of wasted heart values, five diamonds could be too high. On the other hand, six diamonds could be cold. I would try a three heart cue bid, or perhaps jump to four hearts showing good diamonds plus short hearts.

LHO	Partner	RHO	You
1♠	2◇	2♠	?

♠ 9 7 4
♡ —
◇ Q J 9 7
♣ A 10 9 8 5 4

There are some question marks here, but the immediate good news is that the opponents are bidding and raising in your three small. This is always a step in the right direction. There is some danger that partner has wasted heart values so your void remains an unclear value.

LHO	Partner	RHO	You
1♠	2♦	2♠	?

♠ 9 7 4 2
♡ —
♦ Q J 8
♣ A K Q 5 4 3

Here, your void has a lot of value. Its strength is now guaranteed since it controls the heart suit immediately and you have a suit which can take care of any additional losers. Partner has one or no spades so you can make a slam, perhaps a grand, opposite

♠ 3	or	♠ —
♡ K 8 7 5		♡ J 9 7 5
♦ A K 10 7 6 4		♦ A K 9 5 4 2
♣ 10 3		♣ 10 6 2

Note that the void is valuable because it *controls* the heart suit, not because you can ruff a bunch of hearts. Your tricks will come from trumps and clubs. Not heart ruffs.

LHO	Partner	RHO	You
1♡	2♦	2♠	?

♠ 9 7 4
♡ —
♦ Q J 9 7
♣ A 10 9 8 5 4

When contemplating how far to bid, you should consider what partner needs for success and the possibility of your finding it in partner's hand. On this hand, you can make five diamonds if he has

♠ J 2
♡ 10 7 6 5
♦ A K 10 8 5
♣ K 2

And you can make slam opposite

♠ A 2
♡ 8 7 5 4
♦ A K 10 8 4 2
♣ 3

The trouble is that you cannot accurately determine if partner has either of these nice fitting hands, or whether he has one of these.

167

♠ Q 8	♠ K 10 4	♠ Q 4
♡. K J 4	♡ Q 8 6	♡ K Q 2
◊ K 10 8 6 5 4	◊ A K 10 8 5	◊ A K 10 5 4 2
♣ Q 2	♣ J 2	♣ 7 2

None of these hands will make a game. Frankly, I would not have over-called on the first two of them. Perhaps, according to your partner's known style, he would overcall. If so, you would have to consider the possibility.

How can you tell what partner has? There are some telltale clues here.

1. The opponents are conducting a strong sequence, so partner won't have more than a minimum in high cards.
2. RHO chose to bid spades rather than raise hearts. This suggests hearts are either 6-4-3 or 5-5-3 with your partner having four or five. This lessens the chances of partner's having length in clubs.
3. If partner has length in hearts, he is likely to have an honor. This lessens the chance that partner will have high cards in clubs or spades where they would do you some good. In spite of your excellent playing strength, you can forget slams. Partner is unlikely to have the right shell, and slam is unbiddable in any case.

Now, in terms of defense, the question arises. Should we be in five diamonds as a save? I suggest the opponents' maximum is not much. Hearts are going to be offside for declarer should hearts be trumps. And if spades are trumps, you may eat them up with a crossruff. Opposite this hand, the opponents will be pressed to make a part score.

♠ 8 2
♡ K 10 8 7 2
◊ A K 8 5 2
♣ 3

Against hearts, you may get six or seven tricks, and against spades, you may get eight. Scary. The opponents have the high cards, but you have the shape and your side is on lead.

I would bid five diamonds since we may make it and also since they may bid on themselves. But since partner won't have any extra high cards, and because they may be in the wrong place, I won't expect it to be cold.

♠ K 10 6 5
♡ A 6 5 2
◊ K 3 2
♣ 8 5

Another typical hand of average plus value which can end up in the ash can or in heaven. On the plus side, you have kings and aces to make up your ten points. Also, you are blessed with major suits. On the minus side, you have few useful spots and no reinforcing honors. Before the bidding starts, you cannot anticipate much future unless partner indicates some strength and a fit.

LHO	Partner	RHO	You
—	Pass	Pass	?

♠ K 10 6 5
♡ A 6 5 2
◇ K 3 2
♣ 8 5

There is a lot to be said for opening light in third seat, but when you do so, certain criteria should be met.

1. If you open light, you will have to pass partner's response. On this hand you can do that and expect to be in a reasonable contract.
2. But what should you open? If you chose 1♠, 1♡, or 1◇, you will hate it if partner raises. I think that a good suit is one of the criteria for opening on light hands and this hand doesn't qualify. I would pass. With luck, my semi three-suited hand may be able to reenter with a double.

LHO	Partner	RHO	You
—	Pass	Pass	Pass
1♣	1♠	Double*	?

(*NEGATIVE showing four hearts)

♠ K 10 6 5
♡ A 6 5 2
◇ K 3 2
♣ 8 5

Good things are starting to happen. Partner has denied opening bid strength, but he has shown competitive values in a suit I like. In spite of RHO's double, I think we may have the possibility of a game and I must consider what partner could have.

Opposite any of these passed hands, game would be a fair chance or better, considering that LHO opened.

♠ Q J 8 4 2	♠ A Q 8 4 2	♠ A Q 9 4
♡ K 3	♡ 9	♡ 7
◇ Q 9	◇ Q J 6 5 4	◇ Q 10 4
♣ K 10 7 4	♣ J 3	♣ K 10 8 4 3

What I am doing here is the age old exercise in optimism known as "putting cards in partner's hand." It is the reverse of determining which of your points are shell points. Instead, you are hoping partner has the right shell. If you could make only one bid here, it would not be four spades. Two or three is your likely limit. Bidding four would be a serious overbid. But

169

since the auction hasn't gotten out of hand, there is room for a little science. I would suggest two clubs. Since I passed originally, this cuebid cannot mean anything except support plus a maximum original pass.

LHO	Partner	RHO	You
–	Pass	Pass	Pass
1♣	1♠	Double*	2♣
2♡	Pass	3♡	?

(*NEGATIVE)

♠ K 10 6 5
♡ A 6 5 2
◇ K 3 2
♣ 8 5

This is a very delicate decision. My choices are three spades and pass, although double is a possibility. If I had better hearts I might consider it. As it is, I don't intend to punish partner for what may have been a light overcall. True, partner knows I have spades and he can yank the double if he doesn't like it, but how is he to know if I have A 6 3 2 of hearts or K J 9 8 of hearts. He might have the stiff queen of hearts and think it was a major contribution.

I think that since my hand is all working or potentially working, I will carry on with three spades. I am a passed hand, so partner will expect this approximate strength with mostly useful values. I make this bid being aware that partner did not bid over two hearts. His hand is not worth rebidding.

What is my hand actually worth?

♠ K 10 6 5
♡ A 6 5 2
◇ K 3 2
♣ 8 5

The spades obviously are quite useful, but they could be a bit better.

The heart ace is facing a singleton, so it is useful. But it offers no value other than to take a trick. It won't combine with anything. If partner's stiff turns out to be the jack or queen, it will be a disappointment and if it is the king, it will be awful. I can't imagine a hand where partner has the stiff king of hearts which will allow us to go plus.

The diamond king looks to be a nervous card which could easily be worth a lot or which could be worthless. Partner is known to have short hearts so he will have some diamond length. This is a big plus for the king of diamonds.

I would prefer to have something like this hand instead of the actual hand.

♠ K Q 5 4
♡ 8 7 5 4
◇ K Q 8
♣ 8 2

This hand would be far more valuable given the auction so far.

Hand A

♠ K Q 5 4
♡ 8 7 5 4
◇ K Q 8
♣ 8 2

Hand B

♠ K 10 7 6
♡ A 6 3 2
◇ K 3 2
♣ 8 5

Opposite say,

♠ A 9 8 7 3
♡ 10
◇ J 10 5 4
♣ A 9 3

This hand would produce four spades easily opposite hand A and could end up with an overtrick against soft defense.

Opposite hand B, game is possible, but it isn't cold.

Continuing

LHO	Partner	RHO	You
—	Pass	Pass	Pass
1♣	1♠	Double*	2♣
2♡	Pass	3♡	3♠

(*NEGATIVE)

♠ K 10 6 5
♡ A 6 5 2
◇ K 3 2
♣ 8 5

Having decided the hand is sufficiently working, I do bid three spades but I have some reservations.

1. The hand has some questionable features, *i.e.,* the heart ace hasn't gotten any better and the diamond king is probably useful, but not guaranteed.
2. I wish I had some diamond spots.
3. Partner may go on to game hoping for a slightly more perfect dummy.

This last point doesn't bother me too much since I expect partner to have heard the auction also. He didn't bid over two hearts so I would not expect him to carry on. But if he does, he will make it.

Partner knows I am under pressure and may have stretched to bid three spades.

Note that while this is a good hand, it is not a great hand. If the auction had been

LHO	Partner	RHO	You
—	Pass	Pass	Pass
1♣	1♠	Double*	2♣
Pass	2♠	Pass	?

I would pass with no second thought.

♠ A 10 8 6 5 4
♡ 7
◇ A Q 7 5
♣ 8 2

Only ten high, but with such a wealth of playing strength, it should be opened. If you pass, you can get back in the bidding easily enough, but you will find it hard to fully describe the hand. You have game opposite

♠ K Q 3
♡ A 10 6 5 4
◇ J 8
♣ 10 9 2

You might not even need the queen of spades.

♠ 7
♡ 8 5 4
◇ K J 8 6 2
♣ A 9 7 3

Five diamonds is quite playable.

♠ K 7
♡ 10 6 5 4 2
◇ K J 8 3
♣ A 4

Six diamonds is OK.

In all of these examples, game or slam ranged from reasonable to cold. Perhaps you can reach one or some of these spots after passing, but it will be much easier to do if you open the bidding.

As a rule of thumb, when you have good distribution with minimal strength, you can afford to open if your strength is concentrated and you have some defensive strength. I would open one spade with the example hand, but would pass with

♠ Q 10 8 7 6 5
♡ K Q
◇ K 7 6 4
♣ Q

This hand does not have the defensive strength or the playing strength of the ten-pointer being discussed. Further, all of the high cards are flawed. Hard to conceive of a sequence where everything will be working. With

♠ A 10 8 6 5 4
♥ 7
♦ A Q 7 5
♣ 8 2

it is hard to conceive of a sequence where the high cards are *not* working. You may end up in a misfit auction, but even so, your aces will be valuable. I would say that the advantages of opening this hand far outweigh the dangers.

No one vul.

LHO	Partner	RHO	You
—	—	Pass	1♠
2♦	2♥	Pass	2♠
Pass	3♥	Pass	Pass
Pass			

♠ A 10 8 6 5 4
♥ 7
♦ A Q 7 5
♣ 8 2

This is the kind of sequence where you will regret having opened. Even so, you are contributing two sure tricks. Your aces are going to be a plus whatever the trump suit may be.

No one vul.

LHO	Partner	RHO	You
—	—	—	1♠
2♦	2♥	Pass	2♠
Pass	3♥	Pass	Pass
Pass			

♠ K Q 10 8 7 5
♥ 3
♦ K J 5
♣ K J 4

Everyone would open this hand one spade, but they would not appreciate the way the auction developed. Three hearts has only one redeeming merit. It isn't doubled. Your spades are probably facing a singleton. Your diamonds are worthless. Only your clubs rate to be worth anything. And only maybe.

♠ A 8 7
♡ A Q J 7
♢ K 5 4
♣ 8 6 4

This hand came up recently in a Swiss team against good opposition. My first thought was that as 4-3-3-3 fourteens go, this was a good one. All the high cards were useful with the diamond king being the only questionable card.

No one vul.

LHO	Partner	RHO	You
—	—	1♣	?

When RHO opened one club, the hand acquired some different flavors. The honor cards became good. The diamond king is now worth more as are the heart queen and jack. Conversely, the three little clubs are a bigger minus than they were originally. But if the auction goes favorably, these three small clubs may become a plus.

LHO	Partner	RHO	You
—	—	1♣	Double
1♡	Pass	2♣	

This hand is going to the dumps and fast. LHO's heart bid suggests the heart king is offside. And it also suggests we aren't going to get a length trick. RHO's club rebid is also bad for us. It confirms clubs for real. If partner does have a club honor, it will be wasted. It won't help us and it will be onside for them.

No one vul.

LHO	Partner	RHO	You
—	—	1♣	Double
Pass	1♡	Pass	Pass
1♠	2♡	2♠	?

♠ A 8 7
♡ A Q J 7
♢ K 5 4
♣ 8 6 4

Hardly any reason to pursue this. Partner's one heart-two heart sequence showed something in the range of five to seven points. There is nothing in the auction to suggest that partner's values are all perfectly placed. Anything he has in clubs will be wasted. Further you have too much in hearts. Trump rich. Also, your shape is the worst. In spite of the fact that spades were bid and raised, they were mentioned sort of after the fact. They could easily be 4-3-3-3 around the table. What high cards you have will be working. But they won't offer any ruffing values and they won't offer a length trick. Pass. A typical hand partner might have:

♠ 10 6 2
♡ K 9 6 4
◇ Q 10
♣ K 10 7 3

Who knows what makes? Three hearts is down and two hearts is not a bargain. Also, partner has a maximum. He could have less.

No one vul.

LHO	Partner	RHO	You
—	—	1♣	Double
Pass	1♡	2♣	Pass
Pass	2◇	Pass	2♡
3♣	Pass	Pass	?

♠ A 8 7
♡ A Q J 7
◇ K 5 4
♣ 8 6 4

This auction has done a bit to improve your hand. The question is, how much.

First, what has partner shown? Since he did not jump originally, he has a maximum of eight. His taking a second bid implies five or more. If he had five hearts, he would have rebid them rather than introduce a diamond suit. I imagine he has four hearts with four or even five diamonds. Partner could have a stiff club, but two is possible. Since no one chose to bid spades, I think partner has three. He is either 3-4-4-2 or 3-4-5-1.

If partner has 3-4-5-1, it will be a weak one as he would have bid either three hearts or diamonds over three clubs.

With

♠ 9 6 4
♡ 10 7 6 5
◇ A 10 6 3 2
♣ 9

he would take the two bids he did.

With

♠ 9 6 4
♡ K 8 6 5
◇ A 9 6 3 2
♣ 9

he would certainly have bid something after three clubs.

What is clear is that if partner has a stiff club, three hearts will be a reasonable spot. If the defense is soft, three hearts could make an overtrick.

If partner has a doubleton club, he will be 3-4-4-2 with a six or seven count.

It is harder to judge this position. Partner could have something wasted in clubs. Even if he has nothing wasted, it may be hard to overcome two club losers. Partner could not be accused of overbidding with either of these hands, and there is no play for three hearts given decent defense.

♠ J 4 2		♠ K 7 5
♡ K 9 6 2	or	♡ K 10 8 2
◊ Q 10 8 7		◊ 10 8 7 3
♣ 3 2		♣ 8 2

Does all of this seem like a lot of work? It is. It's also unnecessary. When contemplating what to bid, one of the most difficult and thankless tasks is to try to envision partner's hand. When there has been a cue-bidding sequence, you can sometimes do so. But when the auction has shown "values" only, it is fruitless to guess what partner has. Instead, you should try to work within the framework of what you have and what you have shown. The box principle. Or you should consider what partner has shown, i.e., his box. Partner has shown five or six points with length in the red suits. The question is whether his bidding has improved your hand enough to continue.

Your spade ace is excellent.

Your hearts are excellent although the jack may be wasted.

Your diamond king is good but your helping spots are poor.

Your three small clubs are no longer three losers. This hand does not immediately suggest where winners are coming from, but there aren't going to be fast losers off the go. I would accept a three heart bid although reluctantly. This is a close decision and it is based on these factors.

1. My hand has gone up in value and nothing bad has happened to it. Its value is now enough that it suggests we can make three hearts.
2. There is nothing wasted. The hand is pure. If there were any questionable values at all, it would be best to try to beat three clubs. If I had the same hand with the queen of clubs, I would pass. That club queen worthless for hearts, would suggest that partner was minimum for his bids. Without the queen of clubs, there is room for partner to have a maximum and the opponents still to have their bids.

Also, the queen of clubs would suggest defense against three clubs. If they are going down, it would be a poor result to bid on and go down yourself.

As a general rule, when your side has already stretched to a contract, it is not wise to accept a further push. Only when you have all working cards with no wastage should you press your advantage. On this sequence your partner was happy to play at the two level and he may even have stretched for that effort.

No one vul.

LHO	Partner	RHO	You
—	—	—	1♣
Pass	1♡	Pass	2♡
Pass	4♣*	Pass	?

(*singleton club suggesting a heart slam)

♠ A 8 7
♡ A Q J 7
◇ K 5 4
♣ 8 6 4

Just about the best thing that could happen to you. Partner has slammish values with a club singleton. At this moment, he does not know if his stiff club is an asset. If I have 8 6 4 of clubs, his stiff is sensational. If I have A K J 7, or K Q 8 3, his stiff will be wasted. On this hand, I have what partner needs. Nothing wasted in clubs plus I have maximum high cards. The only minuses are too much in trumps and poor distribution. But overall, the controls and working cards make this a fine hand. I would cue bid four spades or even consider Blackwood.

Some points worth considering:
1. Partner will have five hearts, or more. He would not be bidding this way with K 10 x x of hearts.
2. Since partner chose not to cuebid diamonds or spades, it is reasonable that he has scattered values in these suits rather than concentration in one or the other. This means both the spade ace and diamond king will be of value.

———

♠ Q 10 6 5
♡ A 8 3
◇ J 9 7 4
♣ K 2

An average hand. One ace, one king, etc., etc., one deuce. Not the worst shape, not the best. A hand which by itself has little to offer. One sure trick. Some potential tricks. At least the long suits have better than average spots. What is it worth? The auction will tell. If partner has something to bid, this hand has fillers which will be appreciated. But there are lots of cards which will be worthless if partner hasn't complementary help.

No one vul.

LHO	Partner	RHO	You
1 ◊	1 ♡	Pass	?

♠ Q 10 6 5
♡ A 8 3
◊ J 9 7 4
♣ K 2

The early reading on this hand is that it is going to get better. We have a fit. The heart ace has more value than, say, the diamond ace. Partner's mild announcement of strength offers the delicate inference that the spade and club honors can become useful. Before partner acted, the possibility existed that he was broke. If so, your high cards were likely of little value offensively and could be worthless defensively. Partner's bid says that he has some values which diminishes the maximum that opener can have. For two reasons then, you can hope your cards are worth something. Partner has something, and opener has less.

Of further value to this hand. LHO has some length and strength in diamonds. It implies partner hasn't much in this suit so he may have length and strength of some sort in the black suits. If so, that will add to your black suit values.

Lastly, your doubleton club has value. Partner did not make a takeout double. This implies lack of interest in spades so there is the possibility he has some club length. This would make your doubleton club more valuable than if it faced a doubleton in partner's hand.

It is very important to note that thus far, nothing is definitive. There have been a number of general inferences and they lead to general conclusions.

Only as the auction continues will you be able to tell fact from fiction.

LHO	Partner	RHO	You
1 ◊	1 ♡	Pass	?

♠ Q 10 6 5
♡ A 8 3
◊ J 9 7 4
♣ K 2

RHO's pass is a good sign. It is not likely he is making a penalty pass (if they are using negative doubles). RHO is probably broke, or near to it. The importance of this is that the auction provides no reason for pessimism. Partner can have a good hand. The correct bid is either two hearts, conservative, or an optimistic two diamond cue bid.

LHO	Partner	RHO	You
1 ◊	1 ♡	2 ◊	?

♠ Q 10 6 5
♡ A 8 3
◊ J 9 7 4
♣ K 2

This is good news and bad news. The bad news is that RHO has some points. This detracts a bit from the maximum you were hoping partner to have. The good news is that the opponents think they have a fit. This is very good news indeed for these reasons:

1. On this hand, partner will have short diamonds and is unlikely to have a high card there.
2. Partner is sure to have a five-card or longer suit. He would not over-call with a four-bagger if he had a stiff diamond.
3. Now that partner is guaranteed to have short diamonds, he is known to have length in spades and clubs. Your honors are now very likely to be working.

The net of the good news and the bad news is slightly on the plus side. There is another piece of bad news though. It is no longer possible to make a two-diamond cue bid. You will have to choose between two hearts and three hearts, or perhaps a three-diamond cue bid. I think the decision will be based on my knowledge of partner's tendencies. Is he conservative or aggressive?

I would probably go with two hearts. But I would feel guilty. I would pre-fer to cue bid two diamonds and rest if need be in two hearts. Sadly, I can't.

LHO	Partner	RHO	You
1 ◊	1 ♡	1NT	?

♠ Q 10 6 5
♡ A 8 3
◊ J 9 7 4
♣ K 2

That one notrump bid is both surprising and discouraging. RHO surely has a heart stopper, or he thinks he does. Possibly, partner can pick up the heart suit anyway. However, I expect partner to ruff some clubs in my hand which will make it hard for him to play the trump suit for no losers. It is most doubtful he can do both. Also, RHO's bid shows high cards, usually eight or more HCP, or an especially sure heart stopper. Compare with when RHO raised to two diamonds. The raise could have been made on shape values. He might have as little as four HCP. Not like the one notrump call which shows hard defensive values.

This means the opponents have a good claim to the hand. Partner will not have much more than a minimum. We are unlikely to have more than a partscore.

This one notrump bid is all bad news. There is nothing good about it. It does not imply a fit for them so you can't expect your hands to fit either. At least, whatever your expectations were before RHO bid, they have not improved.

I would raise to two hearts or possibly cue bid two diamonds. Since I doubt we are going past two hearts, the cue bid is a futile effort. Perhaps it should be reserved for a raise with better shape.

What I won't do is double. Anytime you have the option of a close penalty double, you should reject it if you have an easy alternative. Two hearts is going to be a good contract if you buy it. And you probably will. Easier to play two hearts than to defend one notrump.

LHO	Partner	RHO	You
1♦	1♡	2♣	?

♠ Q 10 6 5
♡ A 8 3
♦ J 9 7 4
♣ K 2

Nearly impossible. RHO is showing strength so your partner's hand becomes very limited. There is some good news though. RHO hasn't shown any heart strength. Also, your club king becomes more useful. If RHO has merely a good club suit and intends to rebid it, you may be able to make two or three hearts. But if RHO has a typical two club bid with ten plus points, your side has no future at all. Since there is nothing about the opponents' sequence to suggest a fit, you can't expect your hands to fit. You would like partner to have short diamonds, but there is no reason to expect it. He might have short clubs. If he has a doubleton or stiff, your club king will be worth less. Bid two hearts, but don't expect much to come of it.

LHO	Partner	RHO	You
1♦	1♡	1♠	?

♠ Q 10 6 5
♡ A 8 3
♦ J 9 7 4
♣ K 2

Compared to the previous interventions by RHO, this one is rather vague. RHO may have a good hand, but he may have a poor one. From most points of view, things are pretty much as they were before.

Small changes do include:

1. RHO has something more than a pass.

2. RHO has spades which slightly implies short spades in partner's hand. This in turn slightly implies club length thus nudging up the value of the king of clubs.

At this moment, things are still up in the air. One thing is clear. Nobody is going to make much of anything. You may be outgunned, but you do have the first fit.

Since the queen of spades has become less valuable, the hand becomes a sound raise to two hearts.

LHO	Partner	RHO	You
1 ◇	1 ♡	1 ♠	2 ♡
2 ♠	Pass	Pass	?

♠ Q 10 6 5
♡ A 8 3
◇ J 9 7 4
♣ K 2

This raise offers the usual good and bad news. Partner looks to be short in spades. This means your spade cards are useless. This is a bit of a loss. You would much rather prefer that your diamonds were proven worthless. Incidentally, there still remains a moderate chance that the opponents are on a four-three fit. Does RHO promise five for his free bid? Does LHO promise four for his raise? Neither of these treatments are all that good, but some players have such agreements.

Partner's shortness in spades in turn suggests length in clubs and diamonds. The club length is good. The diamond length is bad. The defense may be able to negotiate a couple of tricks plus a ruff. Even if the defense doesn't get a ruff, partner may lose a large number of tricks.

```
                    J 9 7 4
    10 5                              K Q 8 2
                    A 6 3
```

The diamond ten is well placed, but the defense still gets two tricks.

The question now is whether to double two spades, pass, or continue to three hearts.

My own personal style is not to double. You might try it at matchpoints, but I would not. I'm not sure what to lead and even if I did, double would be a close decision.

I would actually be inclined to pass. This may seem inconsistent with the earlier thoughts about jumping to three hearts or making a cue bid. However, on the previous sequences I was entertaining thought of game. Having raised to two hearts, a competitive bid of three hearts will end the auction. We might make four, but we won't bid it. Since bidding game is no longer an issue, I have less reason for getting to the three level.

There are other reasons for not bidding again:

1. Partner may have four hearts only. The auction leaves open the possibility that partner has long diamonds. If so, he might have overcalled with a four-card suit.
2. I have defense to two spades. My spade and diamond holdings are better suited to defending than to playing.
3. Partner heard my raise and he chose to pass two spades. This consideration is especially clear-cut in our partnership. We play that three hearts by partner would be competitive. It would not be a game try. If partner had any excuse for going on, he would have done so.

It is possible that your partner guarantees five hearts for an overcall. And it is possible that you do not use three hearts as competitive. If so, two of my reasons won't be as valid in your partnership as in mine. Even so, the second reason should carry enough weight that you would tend to pass. Actually, three hearts wouldn't be too outrageous, but it will probably lose in the long run.

LHO	Partner	RHO	You
1 ◇	Double	Pass	?

♠ Q 10 6 5
♡ A 8 3
◇ J 9 7 4
♣ K 2

Any time partner makes a takeout double, you will have to take a second look at your hand. There are very few occasions where you reevaluate your hand and find it unchanged. Even when you find the total value to be the same, your individual holdings undergo ups and downs much like the DOW JONES averages. It is only coincidental that a hand is worth the same both before and after partner's double.

On this particular hand, you should have been discouraged when LHO opened. But partner's double should erase any pessimism. The only card suffering from the auction is the jack of diamonds. And its loss is small. Much less serious to lose a jack than a queen or king. By comparison, evaluate the spade queen and ten, the heart ace and the club king. Each of them has increased more in value than was lost in the jack of diamonds. The hand is good enough that you have a close decision between two spades and two diamonds.

LHO	Partner	RHO	You
1 ◇	Double	1 ♠	?

♠ Q 10 6 5
♡ A 8 3
◇ J 9 7 4
♣ K 2

Mixed emotions. You have a good hand but RHO's bid tells you that your obvious trump suit, spades, is not going to break well for you. If RHO has psyched, this estimate will prove wrong, but this is as yet unproven. What is probably happening is that RHO has a weakish (5 to 7) point hand with five spades. He is trying to use his only opportunity to contribute. He doesn't know you have Q 10 x x of spades. He hopes his partner has them. Given all of this, your partner probably has three spades so your game chances will suffer accordingly.

I would double one spade and expect to beat it quite handily. If they run to two diamonds, or two clubs, I will have to reconsider.

Incidentally, there is a convention which will prove useful here. When the auction goes like the one in the example:

LHO	Partner	RHO	You
1 X	Double	1 Y	?

you may find yourself with a good hand with values in the suit bid by RHO. As in the problem, a reasonable solution was to double. So far the problem is quite soluble. And, if everyone passes, you will do nicely. What usually happens, though, is that one of the opponents runs. Say that on this hand, LHO bids two clubs which is passed back to you.

LHO	Partner	RHO	You
1 ◇	Double	1 ♠	Double
2 ♣	Pass	Pass	?

You are going to feel like bidding something. Frequently you will bid the suit which RHO just bid.

Again, what's the problem. Well, the problem is this. If you double, and then bid RHO's suit, your partner will play you for eight to eleven points, but he won't know if you have a medium four-card suit or a solid five-card suit. Since the suit won't be breaking well, partner would like to know whether A 9 7 is adequate support should he have values to raise.

The solution is quite simple. When you have a five-bagger, there is almost no chance that your penalty double will be allowed to stick. Someone will take it out. I suggest that since a double is a futile gesture, instead you should bid the suit immediately. If you do so, partner will know your length is adequate. If you double first, you will have a four-card suit barring exceptional circumstances.

Some examples.

LHO	Partner	RHO	You
1 ◇	Double	1 ♠	?

♠ Q 10 8 3
♡ A 6
◇ 8 7 4
♣ K 9 6 3

Double and perhaps bid two spades if the auction permits.

♠ Q 10 8 5 2
♡ 4 3
◇ A 10 8 3
♣ K 9

Two spades, natural. Note the values are similar to what a jump would have been, if RHO had passed. Two spades is not forcing.

♠ Q 8 7 6 2
♡ K 5 4
◇ 7 6 2
♣ 9 5

I think I would pass. But if the auction allows it, I will bid two spades later. I wish I had better spade spots.

♠ K Q J 7
♡ A J 4
◇ 8 7 5
♣ K 4 2

Almost anything could work. What you can't do, though, is double and follow it with two spades only, *i.e.*

LHO	Partner	RHO	You
1◇	Double	1♠	Double
2◇	Pass	Pass	?

Two spades would be an underbid since partner could pass it. I would choose three diamonds.

Returning to the hand in question.
All fits offer upbeat news when you are reevaluating.

LHO	Partner	RHO	You
—	1♠	Pass	?

♠ Q 10 6 5
♡ A 8 3
◇ J 9 7 4
♣ K 2

This hand offers the usual good news plus a little extra. Both your queen and ten of spades appreciate and your fourth spade adds enormously to the hand's "playability." The club king goes up because partner has opened the bidding. The chances are good that partner has a club honor, but no guarantee. All in all, everything has immediate value except the jack of diamonds. This is normal. Jacks seldom go up or down unless you get some strong definitive information. Partner opens a notrump. Or he bids the suit or the opponents bid the suit. Until you get specific news to the contrary, random unsupported jacks do not do much for your opinion of a hand.

If you play limit raises, this hand would qualify as an average plus example.

LHO	Partner	RHO	You
—	1♠	Pass	3♠
Pass	4♣	Pass	?

♠ Q 10 6 5
♡ A 8 3
◊ J 9 7 4
♣ K 2

Partner has just found the magic bid. Your already nice limit raise has become even nicer. Before partner's four club bid, you were inclined to like the club king, but now, all reservations have been removed. Cue bid four hearts.

LHO	Partner	RHO	You
—	1♠	Pass	3♠
Pass	4♣	Pass	4♡
Pass	4♠	Pass	?

♠ Q 10 6 5
♡ A 8 3
◊ J 9 7 4
♣ K 2

Partner appears to have a minimum slam try. His four spade bid does not mean he has lost interest in slam, but his hand did not improve enough to try again. Your hand, though, has improved enough that you can make another effort. Bid five clubs. Partner made a slam try knowing you had a limit raise and your hand has a completely working shell. You even have the right doubleton. As usual, there is not much point in wondering what partner has. Instead, ask yourself what *your* hand is worth. Considering you have boxed it as a limit raise, your hand is enormous.

LHO	Partner	RHO	You
—	1♠	Pass	3♠
Pass	4◊	Pass	?

♠ Q 10 6 5
♡ A 8 3
◊ J 9 7 4
♣ K 2

Partner's four diamond bid does not do much for your hand. The king of clubs is in limbo, useful perhaps, but unconfirmed. And your diamond holding is soft. I would cue bid four hearts but only because it is convenient. If partner signs off in four spades, I am through.

♠ J 8 6 4
♡ Q J 3
◊ Q 3
♣ K 8 6 5

An atrocious nine count with no future of its own. Only with help from partner will this hand get involved and it won't likely be with much enthusiasm. Hands with queens and jacks have little self worth and this one is no exception.

No one vul.

LHO	Partner	RHO	You
1♡	?		

♠ J 8 6 4
♡ Q J 3
◊ Q 3
♣ K 8 6 5

Hearing LHO open one heart, or for that matter, one of anything, is depressing news. Your Q J of hearts which looked reasonably good no longer does. To make matters worse, you have only three hearts, which suggests they will divide for declarer. Further bad news is that your other high cards are suspect, at least for the moment.

No one vul.

LHO	Partner	RHO	You
—	1♡	Pass	?

Totally the converse. Your Q J of hearts are worth perhaps five times what they were on the previous sequence. Your other high cards are not yet proven, but they may yet be worth something now that partner has shown strength. Raise to two hearts.

No one vul.

LHO	Partner	RHO	You
1♣	1♡	1♠	?

♠ J 8 6 4
♡ Q J 3
◊ Q 3
♣ K 8 6 5

Typical of conflicting news. Your spade jack looks to be worthless, your Q J of hearts are golden, and your club king is suspect. The only card of unchanged value is your diamond queen, and its value is quite unknown. You don't know what the hand is worth, but it ought to be worth something. Raise to two hearts.

186

Note the 'state of the auction' here. Even though both opponents are bidding, they haven't yet confirmed strength. It is still possible your side has a game. It is not likely but the possibility exists.

Both vul.

LHO	Partner	RHO	You
1 ◊	1 ♡	2 ◊	?

♠ J 8 6 4
♡ Q J 3
◊ Q 3
♣ K 8 6 5

Another 'state of the auction' sequence. The opponents' bidding does not imply strength and here, RHO has shown an upper limit of seven or eight points. Compare these sequences.

LHO	Partner	RHO	You
1 ◊	1 ♡	1 ♠	?

LHO	Partner	RHO	You
1 ◊	1 ♡	2 ◊	?

In both sequences, RHO may have as few as four or five high card points. No promise of great strength. But! On the first sequence, RHO may have as much as seventeen. On the second sequence, RHO has no more than seven or eight.

The second sequence, because it is so well defined, allows you to make an accurate evaluation of what's happening. When RHO raises, it is certainly bad news for your Q 3 of diamonds. But the rest of your hand is surviving relatively nicely. Bid two hearts and hope partner has extras. On this sequence, it is a valid hope.

As usual, the Q 3 of diamonds is extremely bad news, given the auction. You would happily turn it in for both or even one of the black ten spots. However, the sequence by the opponents, 1 ◊ -2 ◊ , is so high on your list of good things to hear that you can live with the loss of the diamond queen.

Both vul.

LHO	Partner	RHO	You
—	—	1 ◊	Pass
2 ♣	2 ♠	3 ◊	?

♠ J 8 6 4
♡ Q J 3
◊ Q 3
♣ K 8 6 5

In extreme contrast to the prior examples, this sequence offers nothing but bad news.

1. The opponents have lots of points so partner has a minimum hand.
2. Your diamond holding is poor.
3. Your club holding is poor.
4. Your spade length detracts from partner's defensive potential.

Further considerations.

After a 2/1, you should not overcall on broken suits or hands with unproven values. It is very dangerous. Rather, an overcall should be made when you have a good suit. For instance, after 1♡-Pass-2♣, you would pass with;

No one vul.

> ♠ K J 8 6 2
> ♡ K 3
> ◇ Q 10 5
> ♣ K J 5

and you would overcall two spades with

> ♠ A Q J 10 8 6
> ♡ 3
> ◇ 10 7 6 4
> ♣ 10 2

This is because the 2/1 warns you that your side can't have many high cards. Consequently, you shouldn't overcall with broken suits and broken values because partner won't often have the appropriate fillers.

Therefore, when you do overcall, you will have a good suit with sure tricks rather than poor suits with potential tricks.

Continuing

LHO	Partner	RHO	You
—	—	1◇	Pass
2♣	2♠	3◇	?

> ♠ J 8 6 4
> ♡ Q J 3
> ◇ Q 3
> ♣ K 8 6 5

You know partner has a good suit and not much else. You have enough high cards that partner can't have anything outside his suit. He could have

♠ A K Q 10 9 6		♠ K Q 10 9 7 5 2
♡ 9 5		♡ 9 6 2
◇ 7 6 4	or	◇ 7 4
♣ J 3		♣ 3

Either would qualify for an overcall on the given sequences.

As you can see, your hand does not have much to offer for partner in spite of your trump strength. Pass would be best.

No one vul.

LHO	Partner	RHO	You
1♣	1◊	1♡	2◊
2♡	Pass	Pass	?

♠ 8 6 2
♡ 9 5 4
◊ Q 10 9 6
♣ A 10 4

Not an inspiring hand but one worth a raise to two diamonds. When LHO raises to two hearts, passed back to you, you have a typical competitive decision, *i.e.*, to continue to three diamonds or to pass it out.

If your first impression is to pass, that would be sound. After all, you have raised diamonds and partner has had a chance to continue.

However, a three diamond call is not all that bad for a number of reasons.
1. You have good trumps. This is a 100% requirement for raising and then reraising without encouragement from partner.
2. Your side values are working.
3. Since partner's one diamond bid did nothing to obstruct the opponents, he will have good diamonds or a good hand. His later pass denies a really good hand, but he still has reasonable values.
4. Hopefully, partner has short hearts. If so, he may have some club length plus some club cards. In spite of the one club opening, it is possible your club values will combine.
5. Finally, and perhaps most importantly, your hand is entirely offensive in nature. Admittedly, your shape is poor, but your high cards are excellent. If you had additional garbage cards which did not figure offensively, but which could be defensive tricks, you would pass automatically.

When you are faced with the decision to bid on or to pass, one of your criteria must be to weigh your offense versus your defense.

For example,

LHO	Partner	RHO	You
1♣	1◊	1♡	2◊
2♡	Pass	Pass	?

♠ Q 8 7
♡ Q J 7
◊ Q 9 6 5
♣ A 10 4

This is a far better hand-high-card wise. But it is much more defensively oriented. Your queen of spades may be useful on either offense or defense. But it may prove to be a defensive value only. Your heart strength is a defensive trick but may not have offensive value.

The point of this is that hands with limited, but entirely offensive values may take more aggressive action than better hands which offer defensive potential as well.

If you bid three diamonds and go down, it won't be serious if two hearts makes. Therefore, if you think two hearts can be set, you should be less inclined to bid three diamonds. And, if you are sure two hearts is cold, then you can take liberties in pushing onward.

Both vul.

LHO	Partner	RHO	You
Pass	Pass	Pass	1 ♡
Pass	1 ♠	Pass	3 ◊
Pass	3 ♠	Pass	4 ◊
Pass	4 ♡	Pass	?

♠ —
♡ A K J 8 7 5
◊ A K Q 9 6 2
♣ 8

An excellent hand of unclear value. Game will make, but slam chances are going to require specific cards. Partner will never have Q x x of hearts else he would set trumps earlier. Two small is likely, and a singleton a possibility.

♠ K Q 8 7 5 4
♡ 9
◊ 8 3
♣ K J 6 5

Should partner bid differently?

The main point is that there are far more dummies which will make game high enough than there are dummies which make slam worthwhile.

True, partner can have the ace of clubs, but there is no reason to expect it. And even if so, slam won't be cold.

♠ K Q 8 7 5
♡ 6 2
◊ 8 3
♣ A Q 5 4

Slam is a reasonable proposition, but hardly cold. Notice how conservative partner has been. He could easily have a worse hand, i.e., no ace of clubs.

If you want to try for slam, you can offer five diamonds, but it does run the risk of going down in five hearts.

The main thing here is not to assume the trumps are solid. It is easy to think them so after partner's preference, but they are frequently not.

Both vul.

LHO	Partner	RHO	You
–	–	–	1♠
Pass	3♠ *	Pass	?

(*limit raise)

♠ A K Q J 7
♡ Q 8 7 6 5
◊ A 4
♣ 2

This hand, and the one that follows, point to a serious concept of hand reevaluation.

With partner making a limit raise, game should be cold. And, opposite the right cards, slam can be on. All partner really needs is

♠ 10 6 5 4
♡ A K 4
◊ 10 5 2
♣ 9 6 3

This shell would require three-two hearts.

But partner could just as easily have, say,

♠ 10 8 6 5 4
♡ J 10 4
◊ K Q
♣ K Q 7

in which case game may go down via a heart ruff plus the club ace.

You can try for slam by cue bidding. Partner may oblige, but you may find yourself at the five level before you can stop.

Opposite

♠ 10 9 6 3
♡ 10 4 2
◊ K Q 7
♣ A K 8

Five will be in jeopardy.

The problem is that you have numerous side holes in the hand and partner's raise hasn't helped define where the strength is. Cue bidding may help. But it may not. There is so much to find out about. Which aces? Which kings? Perhaps a stiff heart?

When the bidding goes 1♠-Pass-3♠, opener certainly likes it, but he has no idea how much he likes it. His trumps didn't need much help and now that they have been strongly supported, it is possible his queen and jack may be excess baggage. (See DUPLICATION.)

The rest of the hand is good, but it remains to be seen how good.

Both vul.

LHO	Partner	RHO	You
—	—	—	1♠
Pass	3♠*	Pass	?

(*limit raise)

♠ Q 8 7 6 5
♡ A K Q J 7
◇ A 4
♣ 2

This hand is the same as the prior hand but with the major suits reversed.

Here, partner has raised your broken suit as opposed to your solid suit. And that makes all the difference in the world.

1. Your Q 8 7 6 5 of spades have been 'filled in.' You know you are facing spade strength. On the previous hand, your Q 8 7 6 5 of hearts were of unclear worth.
2. Your A K Q J 7 of hearts are a fine value because they are sure tricks. Perhaps you can discard dummy's diamonds and remove a potential diamond loser. Note that the Q and J of hearts no longer suffer from 'duplication.' See previous hand.
3. You have fewer potential holes thus making the auction relatively easy to pursue.

The important point of these two hands is that when a broken suit is raised, you can see immediate improvement in your hand. When the solid suit is raised, you know there is good news, but you can't be sure how good, or even where that good news is coming from.

No one vul.

LHO	Partner	RHO	You
—	1♠	Pass	2♠
Pass	3♡	Pass	?

♠ J 10 6
♡ 8 5
◇ 4 3 2
♣ A K 6 3 2

With maximum useful points, a doubleton heart, and good trumps, you should continue to four spades. Note that the ten of spades is a golden card. It may not seem like much, but when you have a trump suit of, say,

♠ J 6 2
facing
♠ K 9 7 5 3

you begin to appreciate little extra niceties, like the ten of spades.

No one vul.

LHO	Partner	RHO	You
—	—	—	1 ◇
Pass	1NT	Pass	?

♠ A Q J 10
♡ A 6 5
◇ 10 9 7 6 4
♣ K

With both majors under control, there is no particular reason to remove to two diamonds. Partner's one notrump bid denied a major suit and to some extent it denied diamond support. Your stiff club is probably facing four or five clubs so that suit is unlikely to be a threat.

Both vul.

LHO	Partner	RHO	You
—	—	—	1 ◇
Pass	1NT	Pass	?

♠ A Q J 10
♡ 3
◇ A 10 6 5 4
♣ K 4 2

With partner denying a major suit, hearts are an extreme danger. Rebid either two diamonds or two clubs according to your fancy.

No one vul.

LHO	Partner	RHO	You
—	—	Pass	1 ◇
1 ♠	1NT	3 ♣*	3NT
4 ♣	Pass	Pass	?

(*weak)

♠ 9 7 2
♡ K J 3
◇ A K Q 8 7 2
♣ K

An unusual auction. Partner has a decent hand yet the opponents have been able to push us around quite effectively.

What do we know?

For starters, partner couldn't double four clubs, so it doesn't seem likely that we can beat it badly, if at all. Double would be speculative.

Nor does four notrump seem likely. Before the club raise, there was a good chance that we had clubs stopped. But after the raise, I doubt it. I imagine the club ace is on my left.

Partner has spades stopped, but if his stopper is not headed by the ace, RHO may be able to ruff off a couple of our spade tricks.

Since partner did not make a negative double, he ought not to have four hearts. I expect his shape to be either

	3-3-4-3
or	4-3-3-3
or	4-3-4-2

In all cases, I will find diamond support which will make a diamond contract acceptable and which also will minimize my defensive potential. I would choose four diamonds but would not be surprised to go down two via three spade losers, one club, and perhaps a heart. Even passing four clubs could be right. The stiff king of clubs was never a good card and when RHO bid clubs, it became poor. When clubs were raised, it became worthless.

50 HIGHLY-RECOMMENDED TITLES

**CALL TOLL FREE 1-800-274-2221
IN THE U.S. & CANADA TO ORDER ANY OF
THEM OR TO REQUEST OUR
FULL-COLOR 64 PAGE CATALOG OF
ALL BRIDGE BOOKS IN PRINT,
SUPPLIES AND GIFTS.**

FOR BEGINNERS
#0300 Future Champions' Bridge Series 9.95
#2130 Kantar-Introduction to Declarer's Play 10.00
#2135 Kantar-Introduction to Defender's Play 10.00
#0101 Stewart-Baron-The Bridge Book 1 .... 9.95
#1121 Silverman-Elementary Bridge
       Five Card Major Student Text 4.95
#0660 Penick-Beginning Bridge Complete 9.95
#0661 Penick-Beginning Bridge Quizzes 6.95
#3230 Lampert-Fun Way to Serious Bridge 10.00

FOR ADVANCED PLAYERS
#2250 Reese-Master Play 5.95
#1420 Klinger-Modern Losing Trick Count 14.95
#2240 Love-Bridge Squeezes Complete 7.95
#0103 Stewart-Baron-The Bridge Book 3 .... 9.95
#0740 Woolsey-Matchpoints 14.95
#0741 Woolsey-Partnership Defense 12.95
#1702 Bergen-Competitive Auctions 9.95
#0636 Lawrence-Falsecards 9.95

BIDDING — 2 OVER 1 GAME FORCE
#4750 Bruno & Hardy-Two-Over-One Game Force:
       An Introduction 9.95
#1750 Hardy-Two-Over-One Game Force 14.95
#1790 Lawrence-Workbook on the Two Over One System 11.95
#4525 Lawrence-Bidding Quizzes Book 1 .... 13.95

Prices subject to change without notice.

DEFENSE
#0520 Blackwood-Complete Book of Opening Leads 17.95
#3030 Ewen-Opening Leads 15.95
#0104 Stewart-Baron-The Bridge Book 4 .... 7.95
#0631 Lawrence-Dynamic Defense 11.95
#1200 Woolsey-Modern Defensive Signalling 4.95

FOR INTERMEDIATE PLAYERS
#2120 Kantar-Complete Defensive Bridge 20.00
#3015 Root-Commonsense Bidding 15.00
#0630 Lawrence-Card Combinations 12.95
#0102 Stewart-Baron-The Bridge Book 2 .... 9.95
#1122 Silverman-Intermediate Bridge Five
        Card Major Student Text 4.95
#0575 Lampert-The Fun Way to Advanced Bridge 11.95
#0633 Lawrence-How to Read Your Opponents' Cards 11.95
#3672 Truscott-Bid Better, Play Better 12.95
#1765 Lawrence-Judgment at Bridge 9.95

PLAY OF THE HAND
#2150 Kantar-Test your Bridge Play, Vol. 1 .... 10.00
#3675 Watson-Watson's Classic Book on
        the Play of the Hand 15.00
#1932 Mollo-Gardener-Card Play Technique 12.95
#3009 Root-How to Play a Bridge Hand 15.00
#1124 Silverman-Play of the Hand as
        Declarer and Defender 4.95
#2175 Truscott-Winning Declarer Play 10.00
#3803 Sydnor-Bridge Made Easy Book 3 .... 8.00

CONVENTIONS
#2115 Kantar-Bridge Conventions 10.00
#0610 Kearse-Bridge Conventions Complete 29.95
#3011 Root-Pavlicek-Modern Bridge Conventions 15.00
#0240 Championship Bridge Series (All 36) 25.95

DUPLICATE STRATEGY
#1600 Klinger-50 Winning Duplicate Tips 12.95
#2260 Sheinwold-Duplicate Bridge 4.95

FOR ALL PLAYERS
#3889 Darvas & de V. Hart-Right Through The Pack 14.95
#0790 Simon: Why You Lose at Bridge 11.95
#4850 Encyclopedia of Bridge, Official (ACBL) 39.95

DEVYN PRESS INC.

3600 Chamberlain Lane, Suite 230, Louisville, KY 40241

1-800-274-2221

CALL TOLL FREE IN THE U.S. & CANADA
TO ORDER OR TO REQUEST OUR 64 PAGE
FULL COLOR CATALOG OF BRIDGE BOOKS,
SUPPLIES AND GIFTS.

DEVYN PRESS INC.

3600 Chamberlain Lane, Suite 230, Louisville, KY 40241

1-800-274-2221

CALL TOLL FREE IN THE U.S. & CANADA
TO ORDER OR TO REQUEST OUR 64 PAGE
FULL COLOR CATALOG OF BRIDGE BOOKS,
SUPPLIES AND GIFTS.

Lawrence & Hanson WINNING BRIDGE INTANGIBLES .... $ 4.95
Lipkin INVITATION TO ANNIHILATION .... $ 8.95
Michaels & Cohen 4-3-2-1 MANUAL .... $ 4.95
Penick BEGINNING BRIDGE COMPLETE .... $ 9.95
Penick BEGINNING BRIDGE QUIZZES .... $ 6.95
Robinson WASHINGTON STANDARD $19.95
Rosenkranz
      BRIDGE: THE BIDDER'S GAME $12.95
      TIPS FOR TOPS .... $ 9.95
      MORE TIPS FOR TOPS .... $ 9.95
      TRUMP LEADS .... $ 7.95
      OUR MAN GODFREY $10.95
Rosenkranz & Alder BID TO WIN, PLAY FOR PLEASURE $11.95
Rosenkranz & Truscott BIDDING ON TARGET $10.95
Silverman
      ELEMENTARY BRIDGE FIVE CARD MAJOR STUDENT TEXT .... $ 4.95
      INTERMEDIATE BRIDGE FIVE CARD MAJOR STUDENT TEXT .... $ 4.95
      ADVANCED & DUPLICATE BRIDGE STUDENT TEXT .... $ 4.95
      PLAY OF THE HAND AS DECLARER
      & DEFENDER STUDENT TEXT .... $ 4.95
Simon
      CUT FOR PARTNERS .... $ 9.95
      WHY YOU LOSE AT BRIDGE $11.95
Stewart & Baron
      THE BRIDGE BOOK, Vol. 1, Beginning .... $ 9.95
      THE BRIDGE BOOK, Vol. 2, Intermediate .... $ 9.95
      THE BRIDGE BOOK, Vol. 3, Advanced .... $ 9.95
      THE BRIDGE BOOK, Vol. 4, Defense .... $ 7.95
Truscott BID BETTER, PLAY BETTER $12.95
Von Elsner
      EVERYTHING'S JAKE WITH ME .... $ 5.95
      THE BEST OF JAKE WINKMAN .... $ 5.95
Wei PRECISION BIDDING SYSTEM .... $ 7.95
Woolsey
      MATCHPOINTS $14.95
      MODERN DEFENSIVE SIGNALLING .... $ 4.95
      PARTNERSHIP DEFENSE $12.95
World Bridge Federation APPEALS COMMITTEE DECISIONS
      from the 1994 NEC WORLD CHAMPIONSHIPS .... $ 9.95